T0329007

Cambridge Elements ≡

Elements in Religion and Violence
edited by
James R. Lewis
University of Tromsø
Margo Kitts
Hawai'i Pacific University

MORMONISM AND VIOLENCE

The Battles of Zion

Patrick Q. Mason
Claremont Graduate University

CAMBRIDGE
UNIVERSITY PRESS

CAMBRIDGE
UNIVERSITY PRESS

University Printing House, Cambridge CB2 8BS, United Kingdom

One Liberty Plaza, 20th Floor, New York, NY 10006, USA

477 Williamstown Road, Port Melbourne, VIC 3207, Australia

314–321, 3rd Floor, Plot 3, Splendor Forum, Jasola District Centre,
New Delhi – 110025, India

79 Anson Road, #06–04/06, Singapore 079906

Cambridge University Press is part of the University of Cambridge.

It furthers the University's mission by disseminating knowledge in the pursuit of
education, learning, and research at the highest international levels of excellence.

www.cambridge.org
Information on this title: www.cambridge.org/9781108706285
DOI: 10.1017/9781108613538

First published 2019

A catalogue record for this publication is available from the British Library.

ISBN 978-1-108-70628-5 Paperback
ISSNs 2397-9496 (online)
ISSNs 2514-3786 (print)

Mormonism and Violence

The Battles of Zion

Elements in Religion and Violence

DOI:10.1017/9781108613538

First published online: June 2019

Patrick Q. Mason

Claremont Graduate University

Author for correspondence: Patrick Q. Mason, pqmason@gmail.com

ABSTRACT: In popular culture and scholarship, a consistent trope about Mormonism is that it features a propensity for violence, born of the religion's theocratic impulses and the antinomian tendencies of special revelation. *Mormonism and Violence* critically assesses the relationship of Mormonism and violence through a close examination of Mormon history and scripture, focusing on the Church of Jesus Christ of Latter-day Saints. The Element pays special attention to violence in the Book of Mormon and the history of the movement, from the 1830s to the present.

KEYWORDS: Mormonism, Joseph Smith, violence, Church of Jesus Christ of Latter-day Saints, Book of Mormon

ISBNs: 9781108706285 (PB), 9781108613538 (OC)

ISBNs: 2397-9496 (online), 2514–3786 (print)

Contents

Introduction

Since the terrorist attacks on the United States in September 2001, a cottage industry of scholarship has emerged that explores the "dark alliance between religion and violence."[1] The conversation about religion and violence has become more balanced in recent years by an increased recognition that religion also fuels a powerful strain of peacebuilding, and that a "new breed of religious peacemakers presents a plausible opportunity to advance the cause of peace and stability in many troubled regions."[2] In this outpouring of scholarship and public discussion, however, the religion commonly called Mormonism, begun by nineteenth-century American prophet Joseph Smith, has been curiously absent.[3] *Mormonism and Violence* seeks to orient readers to how this unique strain of American – and now global – religion has engaged the problem of violence over the past two centuries.

Joseph Smith and a small group of followers founded the Church of Christ in upstate New York in 1830; within a few years the body of believers changed its name to The Church of Jesus Christ of Latter-day Saints. The church now claims over 16 million adherents worldwide, meaning there are more Latter-day Saints than Jews around the globe.[4] As a young seeker, Joseph Smith was dissatisfied with the competing Christian denominations in his community. Through a series of heavenly visions he came to believe that true Christianity was lost to the earth and needed to be restored, and that he had been chosen by God as the prophet who would lead that restoration. The hallmark of Smith's early prophetic career was the production of the Book of Mormon, which he claimed to have translated from a record written by prophets in the ancient Americas. Believers immediately saw the book of scripture as a sign that God had initiated a new age of revelations and miracles.

---

[1] Juergensmeyer, *Terror in the Mind of God*, xi.

[2] Appleby, *Ambivalence of the Sacred*, 7.

[3] See Juergensmeyer, Kitts, and Jerryson, eds., *Oxford Handbook of Religion and Violence*; Omer, Appleby, and Little, eds., *Oxford Handbook of Religion, Conflict, and Peacebuilding*.

[4] See Mason, *What Is Mormonism?*

Joseph Smith's aim was to mend the fracture that had historically plagued Christianity, but his new church only added to the spiritual cacophony that characterized nineteenth-century America.[5] When Smith received a revelation for his followers to gather to centralized utopian communities they called "Zion," the movement took on social and political dimensions that antagonized other local settlers. Mormonism was thus forged in a crucible of religious and cultural conflict with its neighbors, an agonistic dynamic that would only accelerate when, toward the end of his life, Smith introduced more controversial teachings and practices such as theocracy and polygamy. Smith prophesied that his church, which he understood to be a proxy for the kingdom of God on earth, would be like a stone that rolls forward "until it has filled the whole earth" and all its "enemies may be subdued."[6] The prophet's audacious claims warmed his followers' hearts but only fueled his critics' suspicions regarding the religion's world-conquering ambitions.

Mormonism has not escaped the cancer of violence that has plagued virtually every religion. Latter-day Saints have generally pursued lives of piety, decency, and neighborliness. But like the devout of every stripe, some Saints have also used their religion to justify and perpetrate deadly violence. They have done so in God's name and believing that they were accomplishing his will. But the same resources that have led some Latter-day Saints to violence – their scriptures, theology, leaders, and history – have inspired others to reject violence altogether and pursue a more peaceable way. In one revelation to Joseph Smith, God enjoins his people to "renounce war and proclaim peace."[7] In another revelation, from which the subtitle for this Element is taken, God informs the elders of the church that, because he will protect them, they are not required "to fight the battles of Zion."[8] By the late nineteenth century, Latter-day Saint leaders had repudiated violence as a live option for believers except when sanctioned by the state.

My analysis of Mormonism and violence is shaped by the theoretical framework established in Scott Appleby's book *The Ambivalence of the Sacred: Religion, Violence, and Reconciliation.* Appleby argues that it is erroneous to

---

[5] See Barlow, "To Mend a Fractured Reality." [6] Doctrine and Covenants 65:2, 6.
[7] Doctrine and Covenants 98:16. [8] Doctrine and Covenants 105:14.

believe "that some kind of transhistorical, transcultural 'essence' determines the attitudes and practices of a religion's adherents apart from the concrete social and cultural circumstances in which they live." This historical-contextual approach means that a particular tradition or movement cannot be reduced to a singular quintessence – thus, popular sentiments that Buddhism is "peaceful" while Islam is "violent" are equally superficial. "Most religious societies," Appleby observes, "have interpreted their experience of the sacred in such a way as to give religion a paradoxical role in human affairs – as the bearer of peace *and* the sword. These apparently contradictory orientations reflect a continuing struggle within religions – and within the heart of each believer – over the meaning and character of the power encountered in the sacred and its relationship to coercive force or violence."[9] Religiously inspired violence and nonviolence should therefore be understood as variable modes of discourse and behavior within internally plural traditions rather than fixed norms.[10]

A brief note on nomenclature is in order. Soon after Smith founded his new church in 1830, outsiders seized upon his followers' belief in the Book of Mormon and applied the nicknames "Mormons" and "Mormonism" to the movement. Rather than being offended, church members, including Joseph Smith himself, largely adopted these terms in referring to themselves and their religion. In late 2018, however, the president of the Church of Jesus Christ of Latter-day Saints, Russell M. Nelson, insisted that "Mormon" and especially "Mormonism" are misnomers that obscure the church's Christian self-understanding, and asked people not to use those terms to refer to the church or its members.[11] This study seeks to respect a group's right to name itself. Since most of this Element focuses on the experience of the Church of Jesus Christ of Latter-day Saints, for convenience I will simply refer to it as "the church." As is customary, members of

[9] Appleby, *Ambivalence of the Sacred*, 15, 27.
[10] See Mason, "Violent and Nonviolent Religious Militancy."
[11] See www.mormonnewsroom.org/style-guide (accessed 19 March 2019); Russell M. Nelson, "The Correct Name of the Church," October 2018 General Conference, available at www.lds.org/general-conference/2018/10/the-correct-name-of-the-church?lang=eng.

the church will be called "Latter-day Saints" or "Saints." I use the term "Mormonism" only when referring to the larger constellation of distinctive historical, theological, political, social, and cultural movements that trace their origins to Joseph Smith's founding revelations. The Church of Jesus Christ of Latter-day Saints is the largest and brightest star in that constellation, but it is not the only one. In other words, "Mormonism" retains utility as a familiar and convenient if imperfect umbrella term for the broad religious tradition, but it should not be reduced to or confused with the Church of Jesus Christ of Latter-day Saints or any of the other denominations or churches whose historical or theological lineage go back to Joseph Smith. Furthermore, "Mormon" is at times a usefully generic historical-cultural designation for aspects that appear in the past but which no longer correspond to contemporary Latter-day Saint beliefs or practices.

This Element traces the relationship of Mormonism and violence in four sections. Section 1 focuses on violence in the Book of Mormon, the most prominent distinctive scripture of the Latter-day Saints. (Latter-day Saints recognize four volumes of scripture: the Christian Bible, Book of Mormon, and two other books of modern-day revelation called the Doctrine and Covenants and Pearl of Great Price.) Readers have traditionally understood the Book of Mormon to embrace a view of heroic and even sacred warfare, though with principled limits on how war should be conducted. But the text also provides a counternarrative that allows for the book to be interpreted as a prophetic witness against the futility of violence. The ambivalence of the Latter-day Saint approach to violence thus originates in the scripture that launched the movement.

In the remainder of the Element, the primary site of analysis shifts from scripture to history. I argue that the Church of Jesus Christ of Latter-day Saints has gone through four stages in its historical relationship to violence: (1) pacifism; (2) active self-defense; (3) assertive and repressive violence; and (4) a renunciation of religious violence and embrace of state violence. These four stages should not be seen as entirely separate and distinct; that is to say, elements of one or more of these differing orientations may appear in a period generally characterized by another approach. Section 2 covers the first two stages and the beginnings of the third, which were prominent during Joseph Smith's leadership of the movement from 1830 until his violent death in 1844. An early commitment to pacifism quickly gave way to a posture of self-defense in the face of the violent persecution that Latter-day Saint settlers experienced in Missouri beginning in 1833. That self-defense morphed into militancy in the mid-to-late 1830s. Though the Saints asserted that their actions were both justified and legal, other settlers and state governments interpreted the martial organization of a religious movement in a different light.

Section 3 addresses the most intense period of Latter-day Saint violence. Frustrated with the local and national governments' failure to protect them from violent persecution, Latter-day Saints under the leadership of Brigham Young employed violent means to secure and preserve the establishment of their Zion in the West during the first decade of their settlement in the Great Basin. From 1847 to 1857 the Saints employed violence as an assertive and repressive tool against Native Americans, dissenters, and "Gentiles" (non-Mormons). This violent period culminated tragically in the Mountain Meadows Massacre, in which Latter-day Saint settlers in southern Utah, along with some Native allies recruited for the purpose, murdered 120 California-bound emigrants in cold blood.

The concluding section employs a more episodic approach to Mormon history since 1857 to demonstrate how Latter-day Saints have come to understand violence as an activity lying outside the proper bounds of religion and exclusively as a prerogative of the state. In the late nineteenth century Latter-day Saints renounced religious violence and came to support and participate in state violence, all as part of the religion's modernization and its accommodation with the American nation. Yet Mormonism has always retained an undercurrent of critique toward state violence and especially war. In recent decades an emergent peacebuilding tradition has flourished primarily in Community of Christ, the second largest "Mormon" denomination, but has also begun to take root in some corners of the larger Utah-based church.

A short Element like this cannot possibly contain all the information that readers need for a comprehensive understanding of any complex religious system. Those interested in learning more should consult the works listed in the bibliography. *Mormonism and Violence* sets forth a series of interpretive arguments about Mormonism as filtered through the question of its relationship to violence. This is not to suggest that Mormonism is unusually violent, or even best viewed through the lens of violence, but only that the religion has a tradition of violence – as is the case for virtually all other religious and secular movements throughout history. Understanding how the resources of a particular religion have been mobilized toward violent ends is an important component in learning what is necessary to counter-mobilize the tradition in the service of peace.

1 "Wars and Contentions": Violence in the Book of Mormon

Many of the world's most cherished scriptures – the Hebrew Bible, Book of Revelation, Qur'an, Mahabharata, and Guru Granth Sahib – present captivating narratives of sacred violence perpetrated by holy warriors or divine beings. The Book of Mormon is no exception. Haunted by violence throughout, the book begins with attempted murder, moves quickly to decapitation and near fratricide, and then spends several hundred pages detailing epic battles with hundreds of thousands of casualties, finally culminating in not one but two civilizational holocausts. Indeed, one of the book's major plot devices is a frequent and often detailed recounting of "wars and contentions."[12] Those who wish to ascribe a violent quality to Mormonism need look no further than its scriptures.

But the Book of Mormon is also a sneaky text. Like any complex work, it is open to multiple interpretations. A plain reading of the book suggests that violence is simply part of the natural order of things, regrettable but inevitable and sometimes even necessary and divinely prescribed. An alternative interpretation proposes that rather than offering an endorsement and even religious warrant for certain kinds of righteous violence, the Book of Mormon can be read as a penetrating critique of the violence that lies at the heart of the human condition.

---

[12] The phrase "wars and contentions" appears, with some slight variations, twenty-seven times throughout the Book of Mormon but not at all in the Bible or in other Latter-day Saint scriptures.

What is the Book of Mormon? Published in 1830 in upstate New York, Joseph Smith claimed that the book was the English translation of ancient American writings inscribed on gold plates delivered to him by an angel. Smith insisted he was not the author of the text but rather an inspired medium who relied on "the gift and power of God" to translate the sacred writings of prophets who lived in the Americas from approximately 600 BCE to 400 CE. It is not necessary here to review the fierce debates regarding the book's authenticity and historicity.[13] What does matter for our purposes is that the Book of Mormon serves as sacred scripture for millions of believers around the world, many of whom read from its pages daily for inspiration, comfort, and guidance.

In structure, tone, and format, the Book of Mormon is most similar to the Bible. Divided into fifteen books typically named after their principal author, its 500-plus pages contain a variety of genres including history, prophecy, theology, exhortation, and poetry. The main storyline follows a family that is warned by God around 600 BCE to flee their home in Jerusalem in advance of the Babylonians' impending destruction of the city. After wandering in the wilderness for several years, the family eventually builds a boat and sails to the "promised land," presumably the Americas. Upon the death of the family patriarch, a recurrent feud between the family's four oldest brothers leads to a schism that produces two warring factions called, after their original leaders, the Nephites and Lamanites.

Violence figures prominently throughout the Book of Mormon. This makes sense because of the ways in which violence shaped the experiences of the book's three primary narrators: Nephi, Mormon, and Moroni.[14] The life of Nephi, whose narration opens the text, is bookended by personal and family violence with broader social and political connotations. His family's exodus from Jerusalem is precipitated by an attempt on his father's life by those who refuse to believe his prophetic warnings that their city is under

---

[13] See Givens, *By the Hand of Mormon*; Givens, *The Book of Mormon: A Very Short Introduction*; Hardy, *Understanding the Book of Mormon*; and Gutjahr, *The Book of Mormon: A Biography*.

[14] This approach is influenced by Hardy, *Understanding the Book of Mormon*.

divine judgment and will be destroyed.[15] After Nephi declares that God has chosen him, the fourth son, to succeed his father as the "ruler" over the family, two of his disgruntled oldest brothers, Laman and Lemuel, assault him repeatedly, and divine interference is required on multiple occasions to save his life.[16] When the family finally separates – both geographically and in terms of their identity – one of Nephi's first actions is to "make many swords" to protect his followers from the Lamanites, whom he portrays as being filled with "hatred towards me and my children and those who were called my people."[17] By the time of Nephi's death, familial violence had spiraled into tribal warfare, with the Nephites and Lamanites engaged in seemingly endless "wars and contentions."[18]

Indeed, war frames much of the Book of Mormon's historical account. One scholar found that military matters constitute approximately one-third of the book's total content, and another identified over ninety discrete instances of armed conflict (not including many other instances of personal violence) throughout the narrative.[19] One twenty-chapter stretch, consisting of fifty-two pages (approximately ten percent of the entire book), is a near-continuous war chronicle that taxes the patience of even devout readers who are typically looking for less martial fare.[20] From a narratological perspective, the heavy emphasis on war can be ascribed to the fact that book presents itself as being primarily compiled and edited by – and therefore named after – Mormon, a military general, historian, and Christian prophet who lived in the fourth century CE. Mormon's life and worldview is dominated by total warfare. He recounts witnessing large-scale conflict between the Nephites and Lamanites from the time he was eleven years old. Four years later, at age fifteen, Mormon is recruited to lead the Nephite armies. His first-person account is a harrowing tale of "blood and carnage spread throughout all the face of the land."[21] Eventually,

---

[15] 1 Nephi 1:20.

[16] See 1 Nephi 3:28–29; 7:16–18; 17:48–54; 18:10–20; 2 Nephi 5:2–5.

[17] 2 Nephi 5:14.   [18] 2 Nephi 5:34.

[19] Nibley, *Since Cumorah*, 291; Sorenson, "Seasonality of Warfare in the Book of Mormon and in Mesoamerica," Appendix.

[20] See Alma 43–62.   [21] Mormon 2:8.

Lamanite armies simply overwhelm the Nephite forces. Hundreds of thousands of Nephites are killed by the Lamanites, until Mormon is one of only twenty-five survivors. Before passing on the sacred record to his son Moroni – the final survivor and record keeper of the Nephite civilization – Mormon offers a haunting portrait of his people's ultimate fate: "their flesh, and bones, and blood lay upon the face of the earth, being left by the hands of those who slew them to molder upon the land, and to crumble and to return to their mother earth."[22]

The bloodshed portrayed in the Book of Mormon is both pervasive and poignant. After one particularly fierce battle in which "the number of their dead was not numbered because of the greatness of the number," the bodies of the killed are dumped into a river and carried out to sea.[23] In the final battle that resulted in the complete annihilation of the Nephite civilization, Mormon documents battlefield losses of nearly a quarter million people.[24] The Book of Mormon also seems to understand that the scope of human suffering entailed in such mass casualty statistics can be difficult to comprehend and even numbing, so it also offers more intimately scaled portrayals of violence. At one point, a group of women and children are burned to death for their religious beliefs, with the missionaries who converted them forced to stand by helplessly and listen to their screams.[25] Near the end of the Nephite holocaust, Mormon reports that the Lamanites took captives of men, women, and children, then "[fed] the women upon the flesh of their husbands, and the children upon the flesh of their fathers." Even worse, in his estimation, was the treatment of Lamanite prisoners by Nephite soldiers, who after raping their female captives "did murder them in a most cruel manner, torturing their bodies even unto death." Mormon spent his life immersed in war, but these atrocities forced him to conclude that his own people were utterly "brutal," "without principle," "past feeling," and "without civilization."[26]

There is a tragic symmetry to the violence that defines the Nephite civilization. Culminating in mass slaughter, it originates with a single killing. After leaving Jerusalem, Nephi and his brothers are sent back to the

[22] Mormon 6:15. [23] Alma 44:21. [24] Mormon 6:11–15. [25] Alma 14:8–10.
[26] Moroni 9:8–11, 19–20.

city by their father to retrieve a collection of sacred records. The owner of the records, named Laban, refuses the brothers' request and sends his guards after them. Undaunted, Nephi sneaks back into the city under cover of darkness and fortuitously discovers Laban passed out drunk in the street. Nephi's gaze is drawn to Laban's sword – "the workmanship thereof was exceedingly fine, and . . . the blade thereof was of the most precious steel" – when he is suddenly "constrained by the Spirit" to kill Laban. Nephi initially fights the urge, recoiling at the suggestion that he should take a life. But the voice whispering in his ear is insistent, reasoning that "the Lord slayeth the wicked to bring forth his righteous purposes" and "it is better that one man should perish than that a nation should dwindle and perish in unbelief." Nephi overcomes his initial resistance and obeys. He decapitates Laban with his own sword, then dons the dead man's clothing to fool Laban's servant and retrieve the records.[27] Rather than leaving the weapon at the scene of the crime, Nephi carries it with him into the wilderness and eventually across the ocean. The "sword of Laban" appears recurrently in the Book of Mormon narrative – first as a pattern to forge more weapons, then as an emblem of kingly power and authority.[28]

Placed right at the beginning of the book, the story of Nephi killing Laban is well-known by Latter-day Saints and other Book of Mormon readers. Most official or otherwise sympathetic Latter-day Saint interpretations ignore the ethical questions associated with Nephi's violence, turning it instead into a moral lesson – Nephi faithfully obeyed God's Spirit even when it demanded a hard thing of him – or accepting the utilitarian argument that the long-term benefits of Nephi retrieving the sacred records

---

[27] 1 Nephi 4, quotes from verses 9–13.

[28] The sword of Laban also figured in the modern Mormon imagination. Joseph Smith claimed that the sword was buried in the box with the golden plates, and some early Mormon converts, in fits of religious ecstasy, pretended "that they had the sword of Laban, and would wield it as expert as a light dragoon." See Doctrine and Covenants 17:1; "John Whitmer, History, 1831–circa 1847," p. 26, *The Joseph Smith Papers*, www.josephsmithpapers.org/paper-summary/john-whitmer-history-1831-circa-1847/30.

outweighed the downside of killing Laban.[29] Other authors have been more critical, recognizing that the narrator Nephi wrote his account of the episode decades after the fact and may have framed his reminiscence to rationalize his actions or place them in a larger storyline justifying his own rulership.[30] For most readers the debate over whether Nephi was justified in killing Laban is an abstraction. But the story took on tragic dimensions when applied concretely in 1984 by Ron and Dan Lafferty, brothers who were members of a Mormon offshoot group. Ron claimed to receive a revelation saying that Dan was "like unto Nephi of old" because of his willingness to do anything that God asked. When another revelation instructed Dan that he was supposed to kill his sister-in-law and her baby daughter, he dutifully obeyed and mercilessly executed both of them. Dan believed that if he wanted to be blessed by God like Nephi then he had to be strictly obedient to God's commands just like Nephi.[31]

The Lafferty murders were clearly exceptional, but they demonstrate how sacred stories have consequences. Political scientist Charles Liebman argued that when the moderating influences of communal structures and institutions are stripped away or rejected, then religious narratives and legal prescriptions can more likely be taken by individuals or groups to their extreme logical ends.[32] Indeed, the animating question for author Jon Krakauer in his bestselling book *Under the Banner of Heaven*, which documents the Lafferty murders, is whether revealed religion is itself dangerous. Krakauer supposes that "faith is the very antithesis of reason, injudiciousness a crucial component of spiritual devotion ... Common sense is no match for the voice of God."[33]

Read in a certain way, the Book of Mormon can suggest that violence is sometimes God's preferred way of getting things done. And God doesn't

---

[29] See *Book of Mormon Student Manual*, 16; Boyce, *Even unto Bloodshed*, 126–128, 169–170, 176–179.

[30] See England, *Making Peace*, 131–154; Hardy, *Understanding the Book of Mormon*, 16–23; Madson, "A Non-Violent Reading of the Book of Mormon."

[31] Krakauer, *Under the Banner of Heaven*, 187.

[32] Liebman, "Extremism as a Religious Norm."

[33] Krakauer, *Under the Banner of Heaven*, xxiii.

just leave others to do his dirty work. The Book of Mormon chronicles extensive natural upheavals that cause devastation throughout Nephite and Lamanite lands at the time of Jesus Christ's crucifixion (which occurs half a world away in Jerusalem). Storms, earthquakes, cyclones, tidal waves, and fires destroy or damage numerous cities, resulting in mass casualties. When the cataclysms subside, the survivors hear God's voice from heaven announcing that he was personally responsible for all of these "great destructions," having sent them as retribution for the people's "wickedness and their abominations."[34] On this occasion, God doesn't just order or sanction violence – he owns it. To date, Latter-day Saints have done little to grapple with the theological and ethical implications of the genocidal God on display in at least this one portion of Mormon scripture.

Although the Book of Mormon seems to justify and perhaps even celebrate certain kinds of violence, even its most hawkish readers will acknowledge that the book does not present unrestrained human violence or total war as positive goods. As noted above, wartime atrocities such as torture, sexual violence, and targeting civilians are roundly condemned as inherently evil (not just strategically imprudent), regardless of who commits them. Furthermore, motivation matters. The Book of Mormon acknowledges that stark utilitarianism and revenge fantasies are not acceptable rationales for violence. Lamanite violence is always condemned as predatory and driven by unjustified hatreds.[35] Nephite violence is portrayed as wicked when motivated by material gain, political intrigue, or religious apostasy.[36]

The Book of Mormon also features the story of a third, separate civilization called the Jaredites. Greed, political rivalries, and a general state of wickedness send the Jaredites into a devastating cycle of violence in which "all the people upon the face of the land were shedding blood, and there was none to restrain them."[37] The Jaredite civilization culminates with the leaders

---

[34] 3 Nephi 8–9, quote from 9:12.

[35] See Enos 1:20; Alma 43:7, 11; 3 Nephi 3:4; Moroni 1:2.

[36] See Mosiah 17:12–20; Helaman 8:26–27; 11:1–2; 3 Nephi 1:9; Moroni 9:9–10, 18–20.

[37] Ether 11:7; 13:31.

of two factions, whose millions of people have already killed one another, facing off in a final death-match: "And it came to pass that when they had all fallen by the sword, save it were Coriantumr and Shiz, behold Shiz had fainted with the loss of blood. And it came to pass that when Coriantumr had leaned upon his sword, that he rested a little, he smote off the head of Shiz."[38] The story of the Jaredites thus renders in dramatic form the sentiment frequently attributed to Gandhi that "an eye for an eye leaves the whole world blind."

If the Jaredite account underscores the futility of violence, other parts of the Book of Mormon seem to point in another direction. Like the Bible, the Book of Mormon never offers anything like a systematic treatise detailing precisely when it is appropriate to use violence or go to war. Any such principles must be gleaned inductively from stories or prescriptions scattered throughout the text. In determining how the scripture applies in the modern context, many scholars have come to the conclusion that the Book of Mormon corresponds broadly to the just war tradition.[39] Developed in classical Christendom by eminent theologians such as Augustine and Thomas Aquinas, just war theory provides moral guidelines that dictate when and why and how it is appropriate for a state to wage war and then places constraints on its conduct.[40]

The argument for a Book of Mormon–based just war ethic draws heavily on the "war chapters" in the middle of the book (Alma 43–62), narrated by the prophet-general Mormon and focusing on the heroic figure of Captain Moroni – not to be confused with Mormon's son and the last surviving Nephite, also named Moroni. Mormon recounts in great detail a decade-long series of conflicts between the Nephites and Lamanites. It is a classic good-guys-versus-bad-guys story, depicting a sharp contrast between the bloodlust of the wicked Lamanites, with leaders motivated by "hatred" and a desire to "gain power" by "bringing [the Nephites] into bondage," and the defensive posture of the righteous Nephites, committed to the preservation

---

[38] Ether 15:28–30.

[39] See especially Boyce, *Even Unto Bloodshed*; Mattox, "YES – The Book of Mormon as a Touchstone."

[40] See Cahill, *Love Your Enemies*, esp. chaps. 4–5.

of "their rights and their privileges, yea, and also their liberty."[41] Captain Moroni is portrayed as the archetypal righteous warrior. The Nephites under his leadership are "inspired by a better cause," fighting not "for monarchy nor power" like the Lamanites but rather "for their homes and their liberties, their wives and their children, and . . . their rites of worship and their church."[42] Bare aggression is frowned upon, as the righteous followers of God are "taught never to give an offense yea, and never to raise the sword except it were against an enemy, except it were to preserve their lives." Furthermore, even those engaging in justified self-defense – to protect their freedoms and prevent their wives and children from being "massacred by the barbarous cruelty" of their enemies – should be reluctant fighters, "sorry to take up arms . . . because they did not delight in the shedding of blood."[43] Although both Nephites and Lamanites are knee-deep in blood, their similar actions are portrayed as morally distinct because their motivations and dispositions are so different. The Book of Mormon insists on pure motives, strongly associating right action with right intention, which is one of the hallmarks of just war theory.

Other authors have argued that the Book of Mormon's provisions regarding the conduct of war are more permissive than classical just war theory allows. Military historian Morgan Deane points to passages that approvingly describe what he calls an "offensive defensive" strategy used by the Nephites. Defensive measures such as building fortifications are complemented by more offensive tactics and even preemptive actions, such as when Captain Moroni mobilizes his forces to "cut off" what he sees as a building threat among the Lamanites who are being led by a Nephite dissenter. According to this interpretation, the Book of Mormon lends support not only to self-defense or even just war but also to "an active defense and interventionist foreign policy" resonant with the so-called Bush Doctrine of preemptive strikes.[44]

---

[41] Alma 43:7–9.

[42] Alma 43:45. Book of Mormon scholar Royal Skousen suggests that the phrase should read "rights of worship" rather than "rites of worship," which would make more sense in context. See Skousen, *The Book of Mormon*, 432, 771.

[43] Alma 48:14, 23–24.

[44] Deane, "Offensive Warfare in the Book of Mormon," 30; see Alma 46:30–32.

In the midst of all these "wars and contentions," the Book of Mormon also features a recurrent nonviolent counternarrative as well as an internal critique of much of the violence that pervades the book's pages. Numerous authors have concluded that in fact the Book of Mormon should be understood as "an anti-war text."[45] How can this be, when so much of the book is dedicated to war stories, some of the book's major heroes (such as Captain Moroni) are warriors, and the book's three narrators (Nephi, Mormon, and Moroni) all relied on the sword as well as the pen? The claim that the Book of Mormon's message is essentially nonviolent usually rests on one or more of four discrete but overlapping arguments.

First, the climax of the Book of Mormon comes about two-thirds of the way through the narrative, when the resurrected Jesus Christ descends from heaven and visits the Nephites and Lamanites who survived the cataclysms at the time of his crucifixion. Jesus repeats to them almost verbatim the Sermon on the Mount, including the passages that have long inspired Christian pacifism:

> And blessed are all the peacemakers, for they shall be called the children of God . . .
>
> And behold, it is written, an eye for an eye, and a tooth for a tooth; But I say unto you, that ye shall not resist evil, but whosoever shall smite thee on thy right cheek, turn to him the other also . . .
>
> And behold it is written also, that thou shalt love thy neighbor and hate thine enemy; But behold I say unto you, love your enemies, bless them that curse you, do good to them that hate you, and pray for them who despitefully use you and persecute you.[46]

---

[45] Madson, "A Non-Violent Reading of the Book of Mormon," 14. See also Mason, Pulsipher, and Bushman, *War and Peace in Our Time*, 1–12 and 57–79; Nibley, "Warfare and the Book of Mormon"; and England, *Making Peace*.

[46] 3 Nephi 12:9, 38–39, 43–44.

In the wake of Jesus's visitation all of the people take his teachings literally, and the wars between the Nephites and Lamanites cease. For four generations, or some two hundred years, "there was no contention in the land, because of the love of God which did dwell in the hearts of the people."[47] A stringent application of Jesus's nonviolent teachings transforms their society and brings lasting peace, prosperity, and happiness, far outstripping any temporary ceasefire secured by military means elsewhere in the narrative.

The second argument for the Book of Mormon as a nonviolent text centers on the story of the Anti-Nephi-Lehies. About a hundred years before Jesus's appearance in the Americas, Nephite missionaries successfully convert thousands of people in seven Lamanite city-states. All the converted Lamanites – called Anti-Nephi-Lehies for reasons not made explicit in the text – demonstrate their change of heart by renouncing their hatred toward the Nephites and literally burying their weapons of war in the ground. Their complete rejection of violence is put to the test when other Lamanites attack their former compatriots whom they now perceive to be traitors. When the Anti-Nephi-Lehies see the approaching Lamanite army, they simply lie down on the ground and begin to pray. Their aggression unchecked, Lamanite warriors immediately start to slaughter the prostrate and defenseless people. Over a thousand of the Anti-Nephi-Lehies are killed before the Lamanite soldiers' hearts are touched by the martyrs' nonviolent moral witness. "Stung" in their consciences "for the murders which they had committed," most of the Lamanite soldiers – more than the number of those they had killed – throw down their weapons and join the surviving Anti-Nephi-Lehies in their repudiation of violence.[48] At the end of his life, surveying the utter destruction of his people, Mormon urges future readers to "lay down your weapons of war, and delight no more in the shedding of blood, and take them not again, save it be that God shall command you."[49] In the final analysis, it seems, Mormon proposes that the way of the Anti-Nephi-Lehies offers the best hope to escape the cycle of violence.[50]

---

[47] 4 Nephi 1:15. [48] See Alma chapters 23–24, quote from 24:25. [49] Mormon 7:4.
[50] For a modern reception history of the story of the Anti-Nephi-Lehies, see Pulsipher, "Buried Swords."

A third argument for the Book of Mormon as an antiwar text focuses not so much on the particulars of individual passages or stories but rather on the book's overall message and character. This literary approach to the scripture suggests that the Book of Mormon is constructed as a meta-narrative exhorting readers to realize that war is futile. The book's many apparent endorsements of violence must be read in light of its profound costs, particularly the seemingly endless cycle of vengeance and retribution that ultimately spirals downward to the complete destruction of the Nephite and Jaredite civilizations. In author Joshua Madson's view, "the Book of Mormon is a witness in confirming that those who live by the sword die by the sword, and that violence begets violence."[51] Hugh Nibley, a preeminent twentieth-century Latter-day Saint scholar of ancient scripture, similarly argued that the Book of Mormon narrators portrayed war as "nasty, brutalizing, wasteful, dirty, degrading, fatiguing, foolish, immoral, and above all unnecessary."[52] Read this way, the Book of Mormon becomes a powerful scriptural embodiment of Martin Luther King Jr.'s assertion that "violence, even in self-defense, creates more problems than it solves" in that it "only multiplies the existence of violence and bitterness in the universe."[53]

A fourth approach comes by way of feminist critique and reimaginings. In her provocative article "Could Feminism Have Saved the Nephites?" author and playwright Carol Lynn Pearson connects the Book of Mormon's militarism to the Nephites' remarkable lack of attention to female voices and experiences. Pearson proposes that "a society that negates femaleness will likely be a society that is militaristic," or vice versa, and that "the Nephite view of women may have been one of the many things that led to their downfall."[54] Women are rarely mentioned in the Book of Mormon in any respect. In the book's many war stories women are virtually invisible, briefly appearing to play only two roles: sending their sons to battle, or

---

[51] Madson, "A Non-Violent Reading of the Book of Mormon," 27. For an extended rebuttal, see Boyce, *Even unto Bloodshed*, chaps. 8–9.

[52] Nibley, *Since Cumorah*, 291–292. [53] King, *I Have a Dream*, 130.

[54] Pearson, "Could Feminism Have Saved the Nephites?" 32, 39.

suffering as voiceless victims.[55] The book often associates masculinity and violence, a fact communicated subconsciously to Latter-day Saint children who play with various sword-, spear-, or bow-bearing Book of Mormon action figures, all of whom are male.[56] A feminist critique of the book's masculinist militarism (or militaristic masculinity) destabilizes assumptions that the violence described at great length in the Book of Mormon is laudable or virtuous, thus providing the moral, ethical, and theological foundations for a nonviolent reinterpretation of the text.

Those who promote various nonviolent readings of the Book of Mormon have to confess that to date their views have had relatively little purchase within the Church of Jesus Christ of Latter-day Saints. The situation is somewhat different within Community of Christ, a historic denominational cousin that in recent decades has divested itself of many of the doctrinally distinctive elements of the restoration tradition and moved instead toward liberal-ecumenical Protestant Christianity.[57] As part of that reorientation, Community of Christ has embraced "the pursuit of peace" as central to its identity and mission.[58] The denomination's evolution has meant a gradually diminishing role for the Book of Mormon in favor of the Bible. But some voices within Community of Christ have advocated for a greater emphasis on the Book of Mormon as a powerful resource in witnessing against violence and in favor of a Christian gospel of peace. For instance, senior church leader Andrew Bolton suggests that the tragedy of the Book of Mormon's historic reception and interpretation is that its earliest readers, including Joseph Smith himself, did not fully understand the book's nonviolent message, captive as they were to an American culture of violence and their own experiences of persecution. For Bolton, the Book of Mormon is a powerful proclamation of Christian nonviolence that also warns

---

[55] See Alma 56:47–48; Moroni 9:7–10.

[56] See https://deseretbook.com/t/toys/action-figures.

[57] See Bolton et al., *In Pursuit of Peace*.

[58] Book of Doctrine and Covenants 156:5. See also Anderson and Bolton, *Military Service, Pacifism, and Discipleship*.

about the ultimate fate of societies that adopt unchecked militarism as their core organizing principle.[59]

The Book of Mormon is thus contested territory, with proponents of just war, preemptive war, and nonviolence squaring off with conflicting interpretations of what the scripture actually says about how believers should live in and respond to a violent world. Given the multivalence of any complex sacred text, we should not be surprised that the Book of Mormon has inspired everything from pacifism to murder. Like other world scriptures, the book lives in a dynamic relationship with its multiple – and often conflicting – interpretive communities. That the Book of Mormon has much to say about violence is undisputed. The precise nature and meaning of that message, however, remains open to debate.

2 "All Are Mob": Violence in Early Mormonism

Mormonism was born into a world of violence. Less than two months after Joseph Smith and his followers established their new church, President Andrew Jackson signed the Indian Removal Act, initiating a new era of state-sponsored violence against native peoples. Five years later, a South Carolina newspaper observed the "unnatural excitement" that consumed the national conversation: "Mobs, strikes, riots, abolition movements, insurrections, Lynch clubs seem to be the engrossing topics of the day." It was not an exaggeration. In 1835 alone, the country experienced 147 riots, most of them in a three-month stretch from July to October.[60] In August of that year the Latter-day Saints' periodical in Kirtland, Ohio, confirmed, "The appearance of our country is truly alarming. Every mail brings new accounts of mobs and riots."[61] Three years later, a twenty-eight-year-old lawyer named Abraham Lincoln delivered a speech worrying what "the wild and furious passions" of "worse than savage mobs" meant for democratic institutions and the rule of law. How could a nation prosper when vigilantes are allowed to "burn churches, ravage and rob provision-stores,

---

[59] Bolton, "Anabaptism, the Book of Mormon, and the Peace Church Option."

[60] Grimsted, *American Mobbing*, 3–4.

[61] *Latter Day Saints' Messenger and Advocate* 1:11 (August 1835): 166.

throw printing-presses into rivers, shoot editors, and hang and burn obnoxious persons at pleasure and with impunity?"[62]

Lincoln could not have anticipated that within a year of giving his speech, his fellow Illinoisans would open their arms to thousands of Latter-day Saint refugees fleeing not only "savage mobs" but also a state government in Missouri that had deemed them to be "obnoxious persons" and authorized their expulsion "at pleasure and with impunity." Though victimized, the Latter-day Saints were not merely victims. They had organized militias and fought pitched battles against their enemies. Five years after the Saints found refuge in Illinois, Joseph Smith would himself fall victim to vigilante violence, though not before commanding his own army, ordering a printing press to be thrown into the street, and issuing a revelation that threatened the destruction of even his own (first) wife if his controversial teachings about plural marriage were not obeyed.

Violence shaped the early Mormon movement in complex ways. Dogged by violence throughout his adult life, Joseph Smith received revelations imagining a godly community called Zion that would be a harbor from violence for all people of good will. In the revelations God affirmed that he would protect the Saints or otherwise vindicate them when their enemies attacked. But when vigilantes threatened Zion's peace, the early Saints resorted to violence, first in self-defense and then more aggressively. Within the space of less than a decade and a half, Mormonism transitioned from a small millenarian pacifist Christian sect to a sizeable church headquartered in a semiautonomous city-state protected by a militia that was a third as large as the entire US Army. This chapter will trace the development of Mormonism's changing relationship to violence during the course of Joseph Smith's life – from pacifism, to active self-defense, to the selective use of assertive and repressive violence. The lived experience of early Latter-day Saints and violence – both received and perpetrated – existed in dynamic relationship with Joseph Smith's revelations accepted as scripture by the church. These revelations not only gave specific guidance for how the

---

[62] Abraham Lincoln, "The Perpetuation of Our Political Institutions: Address Before the Young Men's Lyceum of Springfield, Illinois, January 27, 1838," available online at www.abrahamlincolnonline.org/lincoln/speeches/lyceum.htm.

Saints should navigate a world of violence but also provided a broader millenarian framework that proved to be interpretively elastic enough to vindicate everything from nonviolence to aggression.

"Turn the Other Cheek": Early Mormon Pacifism

The Mormon movement attracted opposition from the very beginning. Though Americans have traditionally prided themselves on their religious tolerance, minority groups throughout the nation's history have often experienced harassment, persecution, and even violence.[63] Most of this religious conflict was merely rhetorical, operating within the spirited but generally nonviolent intramural disputes that commonly occurred between denominational rivals in an increasingly crowded religious marketplace. But the age of democracy in antebellum America cut both ways for religious minorities like the Saints, offering them unfettered opportunities to share their new ideas and gain converts but also celebrating the doctrine of "popular sovereignty" that mobs and vigilantes used to rationalize (and get away with) their attacks on unwanted elements within their communities.[64]

The very day that Joseph Smith reported retrieving the gold plates from the hill near his home, a group of men attacked him in an attempt to steal the unearthed treasure. One assailant gave Smith "a heavy blow with a gun," another a "severe stroke," but Smith was able to fight off his pursuers and race home unharmed except for a dislocated thumb.[65] Constant low-level opposition escalated to the point of physical threats, which led Smith and his small body of followers to leave New York only months after the church's founding. They settled in two frontier outposts that served as the church's dual headquarters for the next several years: one in the northern Ohio town of Kirtland, where missionaries had successfully established a small

---

[63] See Hutchison, *Religious Pluralism in America*; Sehat, *The Myth of American Religious Freedom*.

[64] See Grimsted, "Rioting in its Jacksonian Setting"; Brown, *Strain of Violence*; Feldberg, *The Turbulent Era*; Gilje, *Rioting in America*.

[65] "Lucy Mack Smith, History, 1844–1845, Page [11], bk. 5," *The Joseph Smith Papers*, www.josephsmithpapers.org/paper-summary/lucy-mack-smith-history -1844-1845/67.

community of converts, and the other in Jackson County, Missouri, a lightly settled region on the western borders of the United States where Joseph Smith prophesied that Zion would be established and where Jesus Christ would return at the time of his Second Coming.

Joseph Smith received dozens of revelations in these early years of the movement, eventually published and proclaimed as a new book of scripture, first called the *Book of Commandments* and then the *Doctrine and Covenants*. The worldview on display in these early revelations was ardently millenarian, anticipating the imminent physical return of Christ and the establishment of the literal kingdom of God on earth.[66] Until Jesus appeared, the Saints were commanded to live righteously, preach the gospel, and build a godly society. Any earthly entanglements were a distraction from their real work of preparing the earth for Christ's millennial kingdom.

Many of Smith's early revelations featured dualistic language that starkly contrasted good and evil, righteousness and wickedness, Zion and Babylon. One of these apocalyptic revelations prophesied that the impending end times would be characterized by violence: "wars in foreign lands" and "wars in your own lands." But the Saints were not to participate in the world's conflagrations. Instead, they should "gather," or physically remove, to Zion, "the New Jerusalem, a land of peace, a city of refuge, a place of safety for saints of the Most High God." In a very real sense, Zion would be a cosmopolitan community of peace: "And there shall be gathered unto it out of every nation under heaven; and it shall be the only people that shall not be at war one with another." Zion and those gathered there would be protected from their enemies not by force of arms but rather through God's miraculous power. The wicked would shrink at the divine power they felt emanating from Zion, exclaiming, "Let us not go up to battle against Zion, for the inhabitants of Zion are terrible; wherefore we cannot stand."[67] In his contemporaneous inspired revision of the Bible, Smith included an extended gloss on the story of the ancient prophet Enoch and his people, also

---

[66] See Underwood, *The Millenarian World of Early Mormonism*. Sections of this chapter are adapted from Mason, "'The Wars and the Perplexities of the Nations.'"

[67] Doctrine and Covenants 45:63–70.

called Zion, who lived in a time of "wars and bloodshed" but were protected by divine power.[68] Taken together, Smith's early revelations admonished the Saints to avoid the world's violence and focus their efforts on building Zion, which God would protect so long as they righteously prepared for the Second Coming of Christ.

Smith's revelations increasingly acknowledged that while the Saints might have their eyes set on Zion, their feet were planted here on earth. In August 1831, shortly after Smith first traveled to Missouri, he received a new revelation counseling the Saints how they should go about obtaining the lands upon which they would settle. The revelation presented two options, along with the resultant consequences. The Saints could "purchase the lands," ensuring that they had a proper "claim on the world" that would prevent or at least minimize angry rivalries with their neighbors. Or they could secure their inheritance "by blood." But this latter tactic had two fatal flaws, one principled and the other pragmatic. First, the revelation asserted that God's people were unequivocally "forbidden to shed blood." Second, doing so would inspire their victims to seek revenge, producing a cycle of violence in which "your enemies are upon you, and ye shall be scourged from city to city." In other words, violence might produce immediate results, but it would also precipitate recriminations that would undermine the Saints' own safety and security.[69]

Animated by their literal belief in Jesus's imminent return, the Saints took seriously Jesus's teachings about nonviolence, refusing to respond in kind when attacked. One memorable example came in March 1832, when a mob dragged Joseph Smith from his home in the middle of the night, strangled him, tore off his clothes, beat him and ripped at his flesh, then tarred and feathered him, leaving him for dead. The mob also attacked Sidney Rigdon, a member of the church's First Presidency, whose family had already endured an unsuccessful attempt to blow up their cabin. Rigdon was dragged out of his home with his head bumping across the frozen hard ground until he fell unconscious. Both men were left with chemical burns on their faces after a physician in the mob tried to pour

---

[68] Moses 7:13–18, in *The Pearl of Great Price*.
[69] Doctrine and Covenants 63:27–36.

nitric acid into their mouths. Though Smith and Rigdon survived, Smith's adopted infant son died of exposure five days later because the attackers left open the door of the house despite the bitterly cold weather. In the wake of the assault some church members armed themselves in self-defense, but the church leadership neither issued a call to arms nor sought any other form of retribution.[70]

The Saints' forbearance was similarly tested the following year in western Missouri. Conflict had been escalating between long-time settlers and the Mormon newcomers for two years. In addition to cultural differences – most Missourians hailed from the South, most Mormons came from the North – the Saints were seen as standoffish and self-righteous. Their rapid growth through conversion and immigration meant that the Saints were poised to take over political control of the county. In July 1833 the non-Mormon residents of Jackson County decided to implement forceful measures to rid their community of the unwanted Mormons. In so doing they were embodying the ethos of American vigilantism, which as historian Richard Maxwell Brown observes was traditionally "socially conservative . . . dedicated to the defense of the traditional structure and values of the local community."[71] Acting in the typical style of "respectable" frontier vigilantes, the assembled mob published a manifesto, with names proudly affixed, in which they claimed to be acting out of self-preservation. The manifesto listed various reasons why it was incumbent for local citizens to "rid our society" – "peaceably if we can, forcibly if we must" – of the swarming Mormon "fanatics," including their supposed poverty, tampering with slaves, and blasphemy.[72] Having stated their case, the mob proceeded to demolish the Saints' printing press and the home of editor William W. Phelps, destroy nearly all the copies of the *Book of Commandments*, then tar and feather church bishop Edward Partridge and a handful of others. Under duress, the church's local leadership agreed to a peaceful settlement in which the Saints would vacate the county early the next year.

---

[70] See Staker, *Hearken, O Ye People*, chap. 27, 371 n. 91.

[71] Brown, *Strain of Violence*, vii.

[72] "The Manifesto of the Mob," in *History of the Church*, 1:374–376. See Jennings, "Zion Is Fled."

Despite the violence perpetrated against them, the Missouri Saints did not initially resort to counterviolence nor did they speak of revenge. This was affirmed by John Corrill, an early convert to the movement who was present in Jackson County that summer. In his account Corrill attested that until summer 1833 "the Mormons had not so much as lifted a finger, even in their own defence, so tenecious were they for the precepts of the gospel – 'turn the other cheek.'"[73] Even if they had not formally settled on nonviolence as an article of faith, in practice the earliest Saints embraced a form of Christian pacifism not unlike the earliest Christians.

"We Have Borne Enough": The Turn to Self-Defense

As his people were being assaulted in Jackson County in the summer of 1833, Joseph Smith was hundreds of miles away in Kirtland, helpless. After gathering reports on the situation, Smith received a revelation that provided specific instructions on how church members should respond to the violence inflicted on them as individuals, families, and a church. Speaking in God's voice, the revelation told the Saints that if they wanted to "abide in my covenant" and remain "worthy of me," they must "renounce war and proclaim peace." The revelation assumed Jesus's admonition in the Sermon on the Mount to turn the other cheek and went even further. "If men will smite you, or your families, once," the revelation asserted, you should "bear it patiently and revile not against them, neither seek revenge." If further offenses came, and the Saints continued to "bear it patiently," they would receive exponentially greater rewards for each successive act of forbearance. If the enemy did not respond positively to the Saints' nonviolence, the Saints were to offer a stern warning for them to cease hostilities. If that reprimand went unheeded, then the Lord said, "thine enemy is in thine hands; and if thou rewardest him according to his works thou art justified." Even in this extreme case of repeated and unchecked aggressions, however, violent retribution against the attacker was neither the inevitable nor preferred path for a Christian. If the Saints continued on the path of nonviolence and chose to spare even their most recalcitrant enemies, the revelation assured them "thou shalt be rewarded for thy righteousness; and also thy children and thy

[73] Corrill, *A Brief History of the Church of Christ*, 19, spelling as in original.

children's children unto the third and fourth generation."[74] This August 1833 revelation taught the church what Mohandas Gandhi and Martin Luther King would later theorize, namely that just as violence can produce a vicious cycle of multigenerational retributive conflict, active nonviolence can create a virtuous cycle of multigenerational reconciliation.

Despite God's injunction to "renounce war and proclaim peace," the Saints' nonviolent forbearance was one of the chief casualties of the expulsion from Jackson County. Church leaders in Missouri petitioned the governor for his help in pursuing justice and restoring them to their homes. After outlining the many abuses committed against them, the Saints wrote, "we have borne the above outrages without murmuring; but we cannot patiently bear them any longer; according to the laws of God and man, we have borne enough."[75] The governor responded noncommittally, recommending that the church leadership take up the matter with the justice of the peace – a cruel irony, since local law enforcement officers were among the principal organizers of the mob. Feeling unprotected by the state and justified by the principles of both revelation and republicanism, the Missouri Saints organized to defend themselves against another round of mob attacks in late October and early November – although some, maintaining their nonviolent principles and perhaps sensing the odds were stacked against them, "doubted the propriety of self defence."[76] The first time that church members actively resorted to armed violence came in a skirmish with local settlers on November 4, 1833. In the exchange of fire, two Missourians were killed and several wounded on both sides, including one Saint who died the next day.[77] Though justified by virtually any measure, the Saints' brief and limited appeal to violence in November 1833 only escalated the conflict.

---

[74] Doctrine and Covenants 98:14–16, 23–31. For a contrasting view, see Boyce, *Even unto Bloodshed*, 255.

[75] Petition from Edward Partridge et al. to Governor Daniel Dunklin, September 28, 1833, in *History of the Church* 1:410–415, quote from 415.

[76] P[arley] P. Pratt, *History of the Late Persecution Inflicted by the State of Missouri upon the Mormons* (Detroit: Dawson & Bates, 1839), 12, spelling as in original.

[77] The *History of the Church* names Andrew Barber to be "the first direct martyr to the cause" (1:431).

Swirling rumors about the Saints' militancy only increased the local citizens' determination to drive them out. Rather than waiting until the next year, as their agreement of the summer had originally stipulated, the local militia, comprised largely of members of the mob, forced the Saints to flee their homes and seek refuge in neighboring counties.

In being expelled from Jackson County, not only had church members been driven from their homes, farms, and businesses, but they had been forced out of the land that God had declared to be Zion, the New Jerusalem where Jesus would return. Joseph Smith received multiple revelations that sought to explain the Saints' suffering and give counsel on how to remedy the situation. A February 1834 revelation precipitated the formation of the Camp of Israel, better known as Zion's Camp, a military-style expedition from Ohio to Missouri of about two hundred church members led by Joseph Smith with the hopes of reclaiming the land and homes that their coreligionists had been violently and illegally dispossessed of.[78] Initial promises of support from the Missouri governor evaporated as he took an increasingly dim view of the armed band of supposed religious zealots marching across his state and inflaming local tensions. Stricken by a cholera epidemic and obviously outnumbered and outgunned by the local Missourians, Zion's Camp disbanded before entering Jackson County. Frustrated in their original design to "redeem Zion," the site of their eschatological hopes, camp members separately made the 900-mile return trip to Kirtland. Fourteen enlistees had died along the way.[79]

Zion's Camp has often been remembered – and was understood by many of its participants – to be a divinely ordained military campaign. This interpretation, however, runs counter to the actual language of Smith's revelation. "The redemption of Zion must needs come by power," the revelation affirmed, but it never stated that Zion would be regained as a result of human force, let alone lethal violence. The only loss of life mentioned in the revelation would come from the Saints' own self-sacrifice, not through their own inflicting of violence on others. There would be

---

[78] See Doctrine and Covenants 103.
[79] See Crawley and Anderson, "The Political and Social Realities of Zion's Camp"; Bushman, *Joseph Smith*, 235–247.

neither holy war nor a crusade to retake sacred lands. "Victory and glory"
would be achieved not by force of arms but rather, God told the Saints,
"through your diligence, faithfulness, and prayers of faith."[80] This restrained
view was reiterated to the camp in a June 1834 revelation given while they
were stalled on the banks of a river still well outside Jackson County: "For
behold, I [the Lord] do not require at their hands to fight the battles of Zion;
for, as I said in a former commandment, even so will I fulfil – I will fight your
battles."[81] The precise meaning of this promise that God would fight Zion's
battles was not elucidated, but the revelations were insistent that the burden of
battle was on God, not the Saints.

Early Mormon revelations never called upon church members to commit
violence nor gave them license to do so of their own accord. Although
the August 1833 revelation did leave room for direct self-defense or for
participation in war when "I, the Lord, commanded them," the stated
preference, even in the face of repeated hostilities and undeserved suffering,
was always for a vigorous Christian ethic of reconciliation, with even death
preferable to committing offense.[82] The "armies of Israel," no matter how
large or "terrible" – and Mormon militias in the 1830s were neither – would
inherit Zion legally and peacefully, and only after they learned to "sue for
peace, not only to the people that have smitten you, but also to all people."
Rather than engaging in retributive violence or believing that violence
would be a means of their redemption, the Saints were commanded to
"lift up an ensign of peace, and make a proclamation of peace unto the ends
of the earth; and make proposals for peace unto those who have smitten
you."[83]

The turn toward self-defense in 1833–1834 marked a decided shift for the
religion not just in tactics but in theology and worldview. Up to that point,
millennialism had exercised a powerful restraining effect on the possibility
of Mormon violence, as it oriented the appropriately named *Latter-day*
Saints toward the miraculous culmination of history in which God would
intervene on their behalf to remedy the persecution they suffered for his

---

[80] Doctrine and Covenants 103:15, 23, 27, 36. [81] Doctrine and Covenants 105:14.
[82] Doctrine and Covenants 98:33. [83] Doctrine and Covenants 105:30, 38–40.

sake.[84] The adoption of armed self-defense thus represented a failure of millennial expectations and the Saints' impatience with God's revealed promises to fight their battles for them. By taking matters into their own hands the Saints implicitly acknowledged that perhaps the Second Coming of Christ was not as imminent, and that God was a little more distant, than they had supposed.

"By Blood": Saints at War

Dispersing to neighboring counties, including one created just for them, protected the Saints after their expulsion from Jackson County and kept the peace in Missouri for a time. But as more and more converts to the new religion streamed into the region, the same dynamics that culminated in violence in 1833 repeated themselves. Matters came to a head in the summer and fall of 1838, when relations between Latter-day Saints and Missourians reached their nadir in a conflict called variously the "Missouri War" or "Mormon War."[85]

With several years of grievances accumulated on both sides, no one cause for the conflict can be singled out. But Latter-day Saint leaders felt even more besieged in 1838 than they did five years earlier. In large part this was because of a wave of dissent that had crashed through Kirtland after the failure of a bank that Joseph Smith and other church leaders had established and publicly endorsed. Smith's critics, including many well-respected church members, denounced Smith as a fallen prophet, which led to a brawl in the church's newly completed temple. The prophet's allies rallied, but the Kirtland community of Saints was broken, and the future of the entire movement seemed uncertain. Smith and his closest advisors, including Sidney Rigdon, relocated to Missouri, convinced that the survival of the church now depended on defending it not only from external enemies but also from internal dissent. Feeling hounded on all sides, church leaders assumed a far pricklier, and even defiant, tone as they abandoned Ohio and

---

[84] See Underwood, "Millennialism, Persecution, and Violence"; Walker, "Sheaves, Bucklers, and the State."

[85] See LeSueur, *The 1838 Mormon War in Missouri*; Baugh, "A Call to Arms"; Gentry and Compton, *Fire and Sword*.

placed all bets on building Zion in Missouri. As early as 1837, when a fragile peace still prevailed in northern Missouri, John Corrill observed that preaching from a few firebrands inspired the Saints with a "fighting spirit," which resulted in non-Mormon residents being "stirred up to anger."[86]

The presence of Smith and Rigdon inflamed tensions in northern Missouri throughout the spring and summer of 1838. They spoke of having been "harassed to death, as it were, for seven or eight years, and they were determined to bear it no longer." Contrary to the revelations received in the wake of the 1833 persecutions, church leaders preached that "it was the will of God that the saints should fight [to] their death rather than suffer such things."[87] While maintaining an adversarial posture toward the "Gentiles," or non-Mormons, surrounding them, Latter-day Saint leaders directed much of their ire toward dissenters within the fold, placing primary blame for the loss of Jackson County and the collapse of Kirtland on these so-called apostates. According to Corrill, who became increasingly disaffected in this period precisely because of the changing tone within the movement, the Saints' leaders taught that dissenters would "destroy the church" if allowed to remain, and therefore needed to be "routed from among them." On June 17, Sidney Rigdon delivered what came to be known as the "Salt Sermon," taking as his text Jesus's teaching in the Gospel of Matthew, "if the salt have lost his savour . . . it is thenceforth good for nothing, but to be cast out, and to be trodden under foot of men." No copy exists of Rigdon's full remarks, but Corrill's summary is plain enough: "dissenters, or those who had denied the faith, ought to be cast out, and literally trodden under foot."[88]

Events unfolded quickly after Rigdon's sermon. Dissenters took the hint and began to flee Mormon settlements. Several penned affidavits that were later used to justify the state's military actions against the Latter-day Saints, which only added to the perception among the faithful that they were traitors to the kingdom of God. In the meantime, Rigdon gave another public speech on the Fourth of July, intended both to celebrate the nation's independence and to commemorate the laying of the cornerstone of

---

[86] Corrill, *Brief History*, 29. [87] Ibid.

[88] Ibid., 30; see Matthew 5:13, Doctrine and Covenants 101:39–41.

a Latter-day Saint temple in Far West. Most of his speech was rousing but nothing out of the ordinary given the occasion. But in recounting the persecutions that the Saints had patiently and repeatedly endured for some five years, something in Rigdon seemed to snap. He finished his remarks with a blaze of spite and fury, using extreme language that the Saints would soon live to regret:

> We warn all men in the name of Jesus Christ, to come on us no more forever, for from this hour, we will bear it no more, our rights shall no more be trampled on with impunity. The man or the set of men, who attempts it, does it at the expense of their lives. And that mob that comes on us to disturb us; it shall be between us and them a war of extermination, for we will follow them, till the last drop of their blood is spilled, or else they will have to exterminate us: for we will carry the war to their own houses, and their own families, and one party or the other shall be utterly destroyed . . .
>
> We will never be the agressors, we will infringe on the rights of no people; but shall stand for our own until death.[89]

Having been victims of America's traditional of extralegal violence, Rigdon and his fellow Saints showed themselves to be astute students, applying the lesson that violence could be used not only as a tool of self-defense but also as a more proactive measure to rid their communities of unwanted elements.

Rhetorical provocations from senior church leaders opened the space for more explicitly violent elements within the movement to emerge. Shortly after Rigdon's sermon, a Latter-day Saint named Sampson Avard organized a secretive paramilitary group that called itself the Society of the Daughter of Zion. Avard drew up a constitution that was similar in many respects to other vigilante charters, though laced with a heavy dose of early Mormon millennialism, drawing in particular on the biblical book of Daniel – hence

[89] *Oration Delivered by Mr. S. Rigdon on the 4th of July, 1838, at Far West, Caldwell County, Missouri* (Far West: Journal Office, 1838), 12, spelling as in original.

the group's nickname "Danites."[90] Almost immediately, the Danites gained notoriety for their intimidating tactics, and they served as the shock troops of much of the Latter-day Saints' militarism over the coming months. Avard wrote a letter signed by eighty-three church members (including prominent leaders such as Hyrum Smith, Joseph's brother and confidant), commonly known as the "Danite Manifesto," that ominously warned prominent dissenters to "depart, or a more fatal calamity shall befall you."[91] Historians agree that Joseph Smith was fully supportive of his people's right to take up arms, even as self-defense quickly morphed into more aggressive activities. That Smith knew of the creation of the Danites is certain, but whether he was briefed on the full scope of their activities is contested.[92]

Escalating tensions erupted into outright violence in the late summer and early fall of 1838, sparked by an election-day riot in Gallatin on August 6. Mormons and non-Mormons mobilized their respective militias, with each side claiming the other to be illegitimate. Both sides looted, plundered, and pillaged the settlements of their rivals. Latter-day Saints (primarily Danites) raided two non-Mormon towns, Millport and Gallatin, burning homes and farms, driving out residents, and stealing property – justified in part by the belief that God had consecrated the riches of the "Gentiles" to the Saints.[93] A bellicose Joseph Smith despaired of receiving justice through formal channels and believed that the governor had given the

---

[90] "Appendix 2: Constitution of the Society of the Daughter of Zion, circa Late June 1838," *The Joseph Smith Papers*, www.josephsmithpapers.org/paper-summary/appendix-2-constitution-of-the-society-of-the-daughter-of-zion-circa-late-june-1838/1.

[91] Letter from Sampson Avard et al. to Oliver Cowdery, David Whitmer, John Whitmer, William W. Phelps, and Lyman E. Johnson, June 1838; reprinted in *Document Containing the Correspondence, Orders, &c. in Relation to the Disturbances with the Mormons* … (Fayette, MO: Boon's Lick Democrat, 1841), 103.

[92] For competing views, see LeSueur, *The 1838 Mormon War in Missouri*, and Baugh, "A Call to Arms."

[93] Historian Alexander Baugh documented thirty-six accounts of Mormon violence against property and fifteen accounts of violence against persons in Daviess and Livingston Counties in October 1838. See Baugh, "A Call to Arms," Appendix F (189–191).

Saints explicit permission to defend themselves. According to one reminiscence, on October 15 Smith told his people that "We will take our affairs into our own hands and manage for ourselves ... all are mob the Governor is mob the militia are mob and the whole state is mob ... God will send his angels to our deliverance and we can conquer 10000 as easily as 10."[94] Albert Rockwood, a loyal lieutenant, wrote his father encouraging him to "come to Zion and fight for the religion of Jesus." The younger Rockwood exulted that "the Prophet now goes to the battle as in times of old ... The Prophet has unsheathed his sword and in the name of Jesus declares that it shall not be sheathed again untill he can go into any County or state in safety and peace."[95]

The short-lived war in northern Missouri climaxed in the last week of October 1838. On October 25, a Latter-day Saint militia led by apostle David Patten, nicknamed "Captain Fear-Not," engaged state troops in a prisoner rescue operation. In what came to be known as the Battle of Crooked River, one state militiamen and three Saints, including Patten, were killed or shortly thereafter died of their wounds. Enraged upon seeing their leader fall, Danites horribly mutilated the body of a wounded enemy combatant.[96] Rumors flew, and the situation deteriorated quickly, decidedly not in the Saints' favor. Two days after the Battle of Crooked River, Governor Lilburn Boggs – an avowed opponent of the Mormons since 1833 – issued an executive order, now known infamously as the "Extermination Order," in which he adopted the extreme language of Sidney Rigdon's July 4 speech and stated that "the Mormons must be treated as enemies, and must be exterminated or driven from the State, if necessary, for the public good. Their outrages are beyond all description."[97]

---

[94] Reed Peck, Letter to Dear Friends, September 18, 1839, manuscript, 45, HM 54458, Henry E. Huntington Library, San Marino, California, 78–79; thanks to Alexander Baugh for this reference. See also Bushman, *Joseph Smith*, 361.

[95] Jessee and Whittaker, "The Last Months of Mormonism in Missouri," 25; spelling and capitalization as in original.

[96] See Quinn, *The Mormon Hierarchy: Origins of Power*, 99, 340 n. 90.

[97] Letter from Governor Lilburn Boggs to General John B. Clark, October 27, 1838; reprinted in John P. Greene, *Facts Relative to the Expulsion of the Mormons from the State of Missouri* ... (Cincinnati: R. P. Brooks, 1839), 26.

On October 30, despite the establishment of a truce between Saints and Missouri settlers two days prior, an unauthorized local militia rode into the Latter-day Saint settlement of Hawn's Mill. Most of the women and children had time to flee, but the men fatefully decided to gather in the blacksmith shop, a roughly constructed building with large gaps in between the wooden plank walls. The militia opened fire and mercilessly hunted down their victims, hacking an elderly man to death with a corn cutter and blowing off the top of a ten-year-old boy's head with a musket. All told, eighteen Latter-day Saints were killed in the slaughter, ranging in ages from 9 to 62.[98] Elsewhere, vigilantes gang-raped Mormon women.[99]

As open hostilities ended, state authorities confiscated the Saints' weapons and charged Joseph Smith and other top church leaders with treason. Narrowly averting execution, Smith and his associates were imprisoned under harsh conditions for several months. With their leaders in chains, and recognizing that their situation in Missouri was hopeless, up to eight thousand bedraggled Latter-day Saint refugees trekked across the state throughout the winter of 1838–39, finding shelter and reprieve in western Illinois. Under Smith's instructions, the Saints prepared hundreds of affidavits detailing the depredations committed against them.[100]

In the final analysis, Latter-day Saints bore the brunt of the violence in Missouri, where vigilante justice prevailed over the rule of law. As one eastern newspaper observed, the Saints were "more sinned against than sinning."[101] Still, though many individual church members were innocent victims, as a group the Latter-day Saints bore much of the responsibility for the conflict. Angry rhetoric by church leaders escalated rather than calmed hostile sentiments. Those same leaders looked the other way or condoned the Danites and other militants in their campaign of intimidation and violence against church members they perceived as disloyal or hostile, followed by their attacks on non-Mormon settlements and militias.[102]

[98] See Gentry and Compton, *Fire and Sword*, chap. 10.
[99] See Radke-Moss, "Silent Memories of Missouri," 70–72.
[100] Johnson, *Mormon Redress Petitions*.
[101] Quoted in Turner, *Brigham Young*, 62. [102] See Baugh, "A Call to Arms," 14.

Though their impulse toward self-defense was eminently understandable in light of the many unjustified attacks against them, the Saints' determination to secure their rights "by blood" only led to the fulfillment of Joseph Smith's 1831 prophecy that by doing so they would be "scourged from city to city" and would lose their inheritance in Zion.[103]

"Outrage and Bloodshed": Nauvoo

Scarred by their experiences in Missouri, upon their arrival in Illinois the Latter-day Saints secured a generous charter from a sympathetic state legislature to establish not only their own city on the banks of the Mississippi River, which they called Nauvoo, but also their own militia. Community-based militias were the norm in early America, but the Nauvoo Legion was exceptional, quickly becoming the largest militia in the state. Estimates place its size in the range of two to three thousand soldiers – substantial given Nauvoo's peak population of around 11,500.[104] Despite having no formal military training, Joseph Smith was appointed as the Legion's commanding officer and lieutenant general. Nervous neighbors feared what "General Smith" might do with his private army, but he never unleashed it. Intended mostly as a deterrent, the Legion did little more than drill and parade even in the crises leading up to and in the aftermath of Smith's assassination in 1844.

Historians' assessments of the Latter-day Saints' experience in Nauvoo diverge widely, so much so that one wonders whether they are writing about the same time and place. Was Nauvoo "a place of peace" for persecuted refugees who simply wanted to be left alone to build their godly community or a "theocratic, militaristic city-state" with a "culture of violence" inspired by Joseph Smith's own behavior as a "bully"?[105] In fact, both interpretations have supporting evidence. Devout Latter-day Saints like Louisa Barnes Pratt remembered "continual hostilities in Nauvoo," but blamed the conflict on

---

[103] Doctrine and Covenants 63:31.

[104] Bennett, Black, and Cannon, *The Nauvoo Legion in Illinois*, 99–106.

[105] Leonard, *Nauvoo*; Hallwas, "Mormon Nauvoo from a Non-Mormon Perspective," 60; Quinn, "The Culture of Violence in Joseph Smith's Mormonism."

internal dissent and hostile anti-Mormon mobs.[106] Many non-Mormons agreed about the undercurrent of conflict, but located its source within the Latter-day Saint community itself and especially the leadership of Joseph Smith. A resolution by citizens of neighboring McDonough County complained that the Saints came to the area "not as peaceable individuals" and that their "lust for civil and political power" was antidemocratic and ultimately "destructive of all peace and harmony." Mutual coexistence had become unsustainable; only the Saints' voluntary removal would prevent "outrage and bloodshed."[107] Other critiques focused on Joseph Smith, identifying him as a theocratic "despot" who intended to secure "unlimited power, civil, military and ecclesiastical." They warned of a grand conspiracy in which Mormons were secretly allied with nearby Native tribes and were planning a race war against non-Mormon settlers.[108]

Smith's increasing power in Nauvoo not only attracted opposition from non-Mormons but also dissent among his own followers who thought he had departed from the original principles of the religion he founded. Several followers-turned-detractors formed their own rival church and published an exposé in the form of a newspaper called the *Nauvoo Expositor*. Mayor Smith convened the city council, had the paper declared a public nuisance, and ordered the press to be destroyed – a bitter irony, considering that the Saints' persecutions in Jackson County in 1833 began with the mob's destruction of their press. With mounting charges and gathering opposition, Smith turned himself over to the state and was imprisoned in the county seat of Carthage, about 25 miles from Nauvoo. The governor's promise of protection proved empty, as a mob with blackened faces stormed the jail on June 27, 1844, killing Joseph Smith and his brother Hyrum. No one was ever convicted for the murders.[109]

---

[106] Louisa Barnes Pratt, *The History of Louisa Barnes Pratt: Being the Autobiography of a Mormon Missionary Widow and Pioneer*, ed. S. George Ellsworth (Logan: Utah State University Press, 1998), 69.

[107] Quoted in Hallwas and Launius, *Cultures in Conflict*, 101–102.

[108] Quoted in ibid., 103–107. On fears of a Mormon–Indian military alliance, see Reeve, *Religion of a Different Color*, chap. 2.

[109] See Oaks and Hill, *Carthage Conspiracy*.

In the three years before his violent death, Joseph Smith introduced some of the Church of Jesus Christ of Latter-day Saints' most distinctive – and radical – doctrines and practices, including theosis or human deification, esoteric temple ceremonies, sealings (sacred marriages) of husbands and wives for eternity, theocracy, and most controversially polygamy or plural marriage. None of these innovations necessitated or precipitated violence per se, but the implementation of plural marriage rested heavily on rhetoric that was spiritually coercive and at times even abusive. Although no women were ever compelled to become a plural wife, critics have claimed that Smith and other church leaders used their religious authority to pressure women into consenting. Though individual accounts vary, the overall picture that emerges is that those who entered polygamy, especially in Nauvoo, often did so with significant anguish, even if they eventually reconciled themselves to the principle and practice.[110]

Perhaps no one experienced greater duress than Joseph Smith's first wife Emma, who except for a brief period of acquiescence strenuously opposed polygamy. When Joseph produced the written revelation explaining and justifying plural marriage, it included language specifically addressed to Emma from God. The revelation, canonized and still published in Latter-day Saint scripture, commanded her to "receive all those that have been given unto my servant Joseph" and to "abide and cleave unto my servant Joseph, and to none else." If she did so she would be blessed; if she chose to "abide not in my law," pronounced God, then "[I] will destroy her."[111] Emma rejected the revelation outright; sources say she either burned the copy presented to her or forced Joseph to.[112] Many contemporary Saints remain deeply troubled, even outraged, by polygamy, although the Church of Jesus Christ of Latter-day Saints abandoned the practice well over a century ago. (Various fundamentalist Mormon groups retain plural marriage as a core tenet.) That polygamy's origins include the divine threat of a woman's destruction – and that such

---

[110] See Daynes, *More Wives Than One*, chap. 1; Ulrich, *A House Full of Females*.

[111] Doctrine and Covenants 132:52–54.

[112] See Newell and Avery, *Mormon Enigma*, 153–154.

violent rhetoric remains enshrined in the church's scriptural canon – only exacerbates their distress.[113]

Early Mormonism puts "the ambivalence of the sacred" on full display. The religion initiated and propelled by Joseph Smith's revelations provided peace, hope, and meaning to thousands of seekers at the time, and millions more since. The earliest converts to the new church were so fired with millennialist fervor that they sought to cast aside all trappings of this wicked world, including its violence. But the early American frontier tradition of vigilantism quickly caught up to the Saints, and they found justifications in both sacred and secular sources to support taking up arms in self-defense. Reaching the limits of Christian forbearance, some Latter-day Saints came to believe that the best defense was a good offense. The religious militarism that resulted can scarcely be gleaned from Smith's earliest revelations, but it nevertheless followed the Saints to Utah after the violent death of their prophet. Early Mormon history thus leaves a conflicted tale of a people seeking to build a peaceful Zion but sometimes turning to violence to do so.

3 "Unsheathe the Sword": Violence in Pioneer Utah

Sherlock Holmes helped introduce the world to Mormon violence. *A Study in Scarlet*, Arthur Conan Doyle's first murder mystery featuring the famous detective, transported readers across the ocean from Victorian England to the "Country of the Saints" in the mountain deserts of Utah. The citizens of the territory live in perpetual fear under the theocratic grip of a cold, stern Brigham Young, the successor to Joseph Smith as Prophet-President of the Church of Jesus Christ of Latter-day Saints. In Doyle's rendering, Young is all too eager to dispatch his secret police – the dreaded Danites – in maintaining his reign of terror. "The man who held out against the Church vanished away," wrote Doyle, and "a rash word or a hasty act was followed by annihilation." Residents live "in fear and trembling," daring not speak a word out of line for fear that their neighbor, or even a member

---

[113] See Pearson, *The Ghost of Eternal Polygamy.*

of their own family, might be one of Young's enforcers and "bring down a swift retribution upon them."[114]

In using Latter-day Saint violence as a plot device, Doyle was in good company. Late nineteenth- and early twentieth-century novelists on both sides of the Atlantic frequently outdid one another with their depictions of the "Destroying Angels" of Mormonism. In works by popular authors such as Zane Grey and Robert Louis Stevenson, Latter-day Saints appeared as stock villains preying on innocent women and eliminating anyone who got in their way.[115] Tropes of the violently lecherous Mormon also found their way into early twentieth-century cinema. Films with titles like *A Victim of the Mormons, Marriage or Death, The Danites,* and *Trapped by the Mormons* screened widely across the United States and Europe.[116] Depictions of violent Mormons still pop up occasionally in contemporary culture, from bestselling books like Jon Krakauer's *Under the Banner of Heaven* (2003) to cinematic flops like *September Dawn* (2007). Such portrayals helped shape a sinister image in the public mind, attributing Mormonism's survival and success in part to coercive tactics of repression against both internal and external enemies.

Unable to resist the combination of religion, sex, and violence, most authors and filmmakers have connected their portrayals of Mormon violence to polygamy. Yet while there was a coercive element to polygamy, as discussed in the previous chapter, most of the historical violence that actually occurred in territorial Utah had other proximate causes and contexts. The most lethal decade in Latter-day Saint history was the 1850s,

---

[114] Arthur Conan Doyle, *A Study in Scarlet* (Garden City, NY: Doubleday & Co., 1974 [1887]), 102–103.

[115] See Givens, *The Viper on the Hearth*; Cornwall and Arrington, "Perpetuation of a Myth." A few relevant titles include Jennie Switzer [Bartlett], *Elder Northfield's Home: Or, Sacrificed on the Mormon Altar* (New York: J. Howard Brown, 1882); Zane Grey, *Riders of the Purple Sage* (New York: Harper, 1912); Robert Louis Stevenson, *The Dynamiter* (New York: Scribner, 1925); and Dane Coolidge, *The Fighting Danites* (New York: Dutton, 1934).

[116] See Olmstead, "*A Victim of the Mormons* and *The Danites*"; Weisenfeld, "Framing the Nation."

when church members used violent force against an assortment of perceived enemies, including dissenters from the faith, non-Mormons whom they considered dangerous or hostile, and Native Americans who lived on land or competed for resources that the Mormon pioneers sought in settling the Great Basin.

A note of caution is in order. To characterize nineteenth-century Mormon society as inherently and uniquely violent would be a misrepresentation. Some contemporaneous claims of Latter-day Saint violence were clearly exaggerations or fabrications. For example, in 1875 a non-Mormon newspaper in Utah reported that Samuel Sirrine had been killed by Danites, but in fact he had simply moved to California.[117] Most Utahans, Latter-day Saint and otherwise, lived in peace with one another, and the church provided the spiritual and structural framework for an orderly frontier society. The remarkable fact that historians can name virtually every instance of violence by church members against their opponents in the movement's early decades suggests the relative infrequence of such episodes. By contrast, scholars who study the genocide of Native Americans or lynching of African Americans admit that their estimates of how much violence actually occurred will always be imprecise given the overwhelming number of deaths and relative lack of documentation.

In other words, the chronicle of Latter-day Saint violence need not be embellished to be tragic. Mormon pioneers participated in the forced displacement and massacres of Native peoples in the American West. Latter-day Saint settlers perpetrated the single largest civilian massacre in American history in 1857. And several of those who fell away from the faith in territorial Utah experienced threats, intimidation, or worse. In short, Latter-day Saints in pioneer Utah did engage in violence, and their justifications for violence were rooted in part in their particular religious cosmology and experience. But most "Mormon violence" can also be understood as being symptomatic of broader trends of frontier violence in nineteenth-century America. Latter-day Saints were never *just* Mormons: they were also American frontiersmen and settler colonists who participated in the

---

[117] "Sam D. Sirrine," *Salt Lake Daily Tribune*, December 5, 1875; "That Danite," *Salt Lake Daily Herald*, July 18, 1877.

types of violence common to those groups. Distinguishing a special brand of "religious violence" versus violence perpetrated by people who happen to be religious thus requires more careful consideration. Focusing on the first decade of Latter-day Saint settlement in Utah – a singularly violent period in Mormon history – will help bring these distinctions into sharper relief.

"Lamanites": Violence against Native Americans

The Great Basin may have seemed desolate to those coming from more verdant regions, but it was not empty when the Mormon pioneers first arrived in 1847. As with other Euro-American settlers in the West, one of the first issues the Latter-day Saints faced as they colonized their new home was establishing relations with the Native peoples that had inhabited the land for generations. If the Saints had been sensitized through their own experience of being persecuted and violently driven from their homes as a result of cultural differences, they did not apply those lessons to the people whose traditional lands they were now occupying.

Nineteenth-century Latter-day Saint views of Native Americans were complicated. On the one hand, Latter-day Saints viewed the indigenous peoples of the Americas as the descendants of the Lamanites described in the Book of Mormon. Church members thus believed the Great Basin's original inhabitants to be the designees of a host of divine promises, destined to play a crucial role in God's plan leading up to the Second Coming of Christ.[118] Yet the Book of Mormon also prophesied that the Lamanites' descendants would be "a dark, a filthy, and a loathsome people," and Latter-day Saints came to view Native Americans through that pejorative and culturally violent lens.[119] Indeed, the Mormon pioneers shared many of white America's racialist assumptions and prejudicial attitudes toward Indians, especially when abstractions became concretized in the competition for land and resources. Historian Jared Farmer aptly captures this "tension in Mormon thought between Indian-as-brother and Indian-as-other; between

---

[118] See Hickman, "The *Book of Mormon* as Amerindian Apocalypse."
[119] Mormon 5:15. See Stevenson, "Reckoning with Race in the Book of Mormon"; Mauss, *All Abraham's Children*, esp. chaps. 3–5.

sympathy and contempt, belief and doubt. Pioneer leaders sincerely meant to *try* to redeem the Lamanites. But first things came first" – and violence ensued.[120]

The first wave of Mormon pioneers in 1847 coexisted warily with the Ute and Shoshone inhabitants of the Salt Lake Valley. But the sudden swell in population led to increased stress on the region's available freshwater, timber, game, and fish. Conflict between pioneers and natives gradually escalated over the next two years especially as Latter-day Saint settlements began to expand into Utah Valley to the south. Brigham Young initially counseled his people to keep their distance from Indians and deal with them fairly. Yet he also believed the relationship between the two groups should be managed on his terms – with Indian allies ultimately under Latter-day Saint control and converting to their religion.

Limited outbreaks of low-level violence in 1848 and 1849 took a significant turn for the worse in 1850, when three Latter-day Saint settlers savagely murdered a Ute named Old Bishop for stealing a shirt. At a council convened to determine the next steps, church leaders adopted an "us or them" mentality. As Young pronounced, "They must either quit the ground or we must ... If we don't kill those Lake Utes, they will kill us."[121] Just over a decade removed from Governor Boggs' extermination order in Missouri, upon the unanimous recommendation of his council Young ordered a selective extermination campaign, with Ute men to be killed and women and children to be saved when possible. The resultant military operation resulted in the deaths of approximately one hundred Utes and one Latter-day Saint. War brought atrocities. At Table Rock on Valentine's Day 1850, Latter-day Saint militiamen lined up a group of eleven surrendered Ute warriors and summarily executed them as their families looked on in horror. The settlers decapitated the Indians' bodies and sent their heads to Salt Lake City for "science."[122] The church's First Presidency temporarily advocated a policy of removing all Indians from

---

[120] Farmer, *On Zion's Mount*, 61.

[121] Quoted in Christy, "Open Hand and Mailed Fist," 226–227. See also Farmer, *On Zion's Mount*, chap. 2; Turner, *Brigham Young*, 208–218.

[122] Farmer, *On Zion's Mount*, 74.

Utah Territory – a grim echo of the Trail of Tears, not to mention their own forced exoduses from Missouri and Illinois. Indigenous peoples were never entirely removed from Utah, but over the next two decades Latter-day Saints assisted federal agents in systematically subjugating and dispossessing the native Ute, Shoshone, Goshute, Pahvant, Sanpit, and Southern Paiute populations. Those who survived were forced onto remote reservations.[123]

Brigham Young did not have the appetite for sustained Indian-killing. In the early 1850s Young, who was not only Prophet-President of the Church of Jesus Christ of Latter-day Saints but also territorial governor and Superintendent of Indian Affairs, settled on a policy that "it is cheaper to feed the Indians than to fight them" – a position driven by pragmatism as much as principle. Nevertheless, outbreaks of violence continued throughout the 1860s, notably during the Black Hawk War of 1865–1868. One of the low points of the conflict came in April 1866, when the Latter-day Saint settlers of Circleville, an isolated and exposed community in south-central Utah, massacred at least sixteen captured Paiutes, slitting the throats of some and individually executing women and children. Even given the fog of war, local settlers' fears, and the depredations committed by Indians in the area, the Circleville Massacre stands out as a particularly ruthless atrocity.[124] Following the conclusion of the Black Hawk War, relations between the Saints and Paiutes on Utah's southern frontier settled into a more comfortable and largely nonviolent pattern, with frequent intermingling and even occasional intermarriage, though by then the regional power dynamic had been well established.[125]

Latter-day Saint violence against Native Americans in pioneer Utah is in many ways easy to explain in its historical context, though still hard to stomach. Quite simply, the Saints acted like other white American settler colonists – first on their own accord, then as willing agents of US government policy. The recognizable pattern of white colonial violence is all the more tragic in Utah, however, given the Saints' distinctive eschatological beliefs about the important roles to be played by the Lamanites in the last

[123] See Smith, "Mormon Conquest"; Blackhawk, *Violence over the Land*, chap. 7.
[124] Winkler, "The Circleville Massacre."
[125] Reeve, *Making Space on the Western Frontier*, 108–109.

days. But while the content of Latter-day Saint "Lamanite theology" differed from the romanticized Euro-American portrait of the Indian as "noble savage," the two mythologies functioned similarly by placing native peoples on an unattainable pedestal. Realities of frontier settlement among the "Lamanites" proved disillusioning for the Saints, as lived experience did not accord with the prophecies of the Book of Mormon. The Indians' resultant "fall from grace" in the Latter-day Saint settlers' eyes touched off a period of intermittent and sometimes intense violence between the two groups that lasted until Utah's native peoples were effectively removed from areas of white settlement.[126] Latter-day Saint violence against Utah's original inhabitants was largely typical of the disastrous history of white–Indian relations on the American frontier, with cultural differences and competition over land and natural resources precipitating conflict, war, and atrocities. Though sung in a Mormon key, the tune of white settler violence was depressingly familiar.

"Gentiles": Violence against Non-Mormons

Like the Bible, Latter-day Saint scriptures roughly divide the world's population into two broad categories: the people of Israel and everyone else, called "Gentiles." Nineteenth-century Latter-day Saints believed that they and a few other groups like Jews and "Lamanites" were all modern branches of the biblical house of Israel.[127] While the Gentiles also play crucial roles in Latter-day Saint eschatology – in the Mormon salvation drama, virtually everyone has a part – in the church "Gentile" quickly became shorthand for the outside world, and the designation eventually came to take on more than a whiff of opprobrium. There were the chosen, the elect, God's covenant people – and then there were the Gentiles. In her study of monotheism and violence in the Hebrew Bible, Regina Schwartz suggests that violence originates in this fundamental act of identity formation: "imagining identity as an act of distinguishing and separating from others, of boundary making and line drawing, is the most frequent and fundamental act of violence we commit. Violence is not only what we do to

---

[126] See Lindell, "Fall from Grace."

[127] See Mauss, *All Abraham's Children*, chap. 2; Shipps, *Mormonism*.

the Other. It is prior to that. Violence is the very construction of the Other."[128]

Imagining non-Mormon settlers as Gentiles had helped justify Danite violence against Missourians in 1838. Latter-day Saint antipathy toward the Gentiles increased exponentially after the assassination of Joseph Smith. The surviving members of the Council of Fifty, which Smith organized shortly before his death to anticipate the establishment of the political kingdom of God on earth, were especially vitriolic in their denunciations. At a series of meetings held less than a year after the prophet's murder in 1844, Brigham Young declared that the Gentiles' "doom is sealed." Because the Gentiles had "spilt the blood of our prophets and sought to kill us off," William W. Phelps said he retained "no feeling of mercy for them." In turn, Young endorsed the sentiments of others on the council who said, "let the damned scoundrels be killed, let them be swept off from the earth."[129] The angry bravado displayed by Council of Fifty members behind closed doors had more bark than bite. But Latter-day Saints had internalized the violence they had received over the past decade and found other ways to project it. Church leaders incorporated into their most sacred rituals a prayer for God to "avenge the blood of the prophets," particularly Joseph Smith. Removed from the church's temple ceremony in 1927, the "oath of vengeance," as it came to be called, was a desperate plea for God to exact retribution on their enemies because the Saints were in no position to do so themselves.[130]

Despite their anger and fulminations, when hostilities with surrounding non-Mormons in Illinois reached a breaking point in late 1845, Brigham Young and his fellow Latter-day Saints signed a treaty allowing for them to leave the state peacefully rather than engage in open warfare. Having opted to fight in Missouri in 1838, in 1845 the Saints wisely – but indignantly – chose flight. When they made their epic trek across the continent, the Mormon pioneers carried not only provisions but also bitter resentment against the Gentile nation that had treated them so harshly. They nursed

---

[128] Schwartz, *The Curse of Cain*, 5.

[129] Grow et al, *Council of Fifty, Minutes*, 257, 285, 300.

[130] See Flake, *The Politics of American Religious Identity*, 82–83; Anderson, *The Development of LDS Temple Worship*, 164, 218.

these wounds over the next decade, and then released their tensions in a spate of violence in the fateful year of 1857. Utah had been admitted into the Union in 1850 as a territory rather than a state, which meant that the federal government sent appointees to fill various posts in the territorial government and courts. The Saints chafed at what they saw as outside interference in their affairs. For their part, most of the federal appointees held a reciprocally dim view of the Saints. Some fielded reports back to Washington claiming that the Mormons were in a state of rebellion against the government, which prompted President James Buchanan to muster a fifth of the nation's standing army to quell the alleged insurrection, precipitating what came to be known as the Utah War of 1857–58.[131]

The Saints received word of the advancing army on the day they were celebrating the tenth anniversary of their arrival into Salt Lake Valley. They immediately adopted a defiant tone. A hastily composed song expressed the expectation, and even invitation, of violence: "Powder Bullet Sword and Gun / Boys arouse we'll have some fun / As sure as fate the time has come / So fix your Guns for shooting." Goaded by Brigham Young, church members saw the marching troops as yet another mob. Apostle Franklin D. Richards appealed to God "for protection against the hostilities of any Mob that shall invade our Territory." Hawn's Mill massacre survivor Charles Jameson ascended the pulpit during a Sunday meeting a week after learning of the army's approach and proclaimed, "I feel like fighting, & if any Mob comes here I feel like giving them the best I have got in the locker."[132] A clear consensus emerged: the Saints would not let history repeat itself, and they would take whatever strong measures were necessary to protect their community from this latest threat.

With the army on the march but still well out of reach, a number of Latter-day Saints lashed out against various Gentile proxies in their midst. In late July 1857, a group of Saints attacked the US surveyor's office in Salt Lake City. They assailed the surveyor with a barrage of rocks and gave an excommunicated church member employed there as a clerk "a tremendous

---

[131] MacKinnon, *At Sword's Point*; Rogers, *Unpopular Sovereignty*.
[132] Quoted in Walker, Turley, and Leonard, *Massacre at Mountain Meadows*, 39, 49, 107.

thrashing" with stones and clubs. Two days later, Latter-day Saint vigilantes hauled a second clerk out of the office and carried him to the nearby Jordan River, where they placed a rope around his neck and forced him, at knife- and gunpoint, to testify against his superiors.[133]

But none of these happenings in July or August, or at any other point in Mormon history, would compare to what occurred in September 1857. A large wagon train hailing from Arkansas, known as the Baker-Fancher party, arrived in Salt Lake City in August and restocked before continuing on the southern trail through Utah territory toward California. Heightened tensions throughout the region contributed to a series of minor confrontations between the emigrants and Latter-day Saint settlers. Rumors spread that the emigrants were poisoning wells and cattle along the way, and some members of the party boasted that they had been in the mob that killed Joseph Smith. As the wagon train passed through southern Utah, local church leaders Isaac Haight and John D. Lee devised a scheme to attack the party and seize their goods while blaming the incident on hostile Indians.

Lee led some Paiute recruits and Saints disguised as Indians in an ambush on the Baker-Fancher party on September 7. The emigrants repelled the initial assault, turning what began as a surprise attack into a weeklong siege. Lee needed reinforcements to overcome the travelers' makeshift wagon fort, and sought the help of William Dame, commander of the territorial militia in southern Utah and the ranking church leader in nearby Parowan. A hurriedly assembled council of leaders sent an express rider to Salt Lake City to ask Brigham Young's advice. But Young's reply, which instructed the locals to let the wagon train "go in peace," arrived after Dame authorized the militia to attack. On September 11, 1857, under a white flag of truce, Lee told the emigrants that the Mormon militia would accompany them to safety, but only under the condition that they surrender their weapons. With their food and water supplies rapidly dwindling, the emigrants had little choice. The militia lined up the disarmed men single file and separated them from the women and children. Upon a prearranged signal, the Saints and their Paiute allies slaughtered some 120 men, women, and children in cold blood. They spared only seventeen children whom they

---

[133] Ibid., 42–43.

considered too young to testify against the perpetrators. The perpetrators appropriated the dead emigrants' property, distributed a small amount to the Paiutes, and returned to their settlements, placing the surviving children in foster homes before eventually returning them to their extended families in the East. Though federal marshals investigated the massacre, and a grand jury indicted nine men for their leading roles, John D. Lee was the only perpetrator ever convicted for his (and others') crimes.[134]

Because the Utah War was mediated peacefully, without major pitched battles between the army and the Latter-day Saints, the conflict has often been characterized as being "bloodless." But as historian William MacKinnon has demonstrated, events surrounding the Utah War resulted in approximately 150 fatalities, about the same number as in the more famous contemporaneous carnage in "bleeding Kansas." The majority of those deaths came at Mountain Meadows, but they also included the killing of a civilian trader named Richard Yates who refused to sell gunpowder to the reactivated Nauvoo Legion, as well as the murder of five members of the so-called Aiken party, who had been suspected of spying for the army or potentially establishing a gambling and prostitution house. Both the Yates and Aiken murders were carried out by men who gained notoriety – and claimed a long hit list – as Brigham Young's enforcers.[135]

How do we explain all this Latter-day Saint violence against "Gentiles"? A general culture of violence on the American frontier and the war hysteria particular to 1857 are essential contexts. Regina Schwartz's observation that violence inheres, or at least potentiates, in the act of oppositional identity formation – the "Saints" versus the "Gentiles" – is also valuable. In addition, we should consider seriously the Saints' own self-understanding that what they were experiencing in 1857 was a recapitulation of what they had endured in Missouri and Illinois. Violence has long-lasting psychological

---

[134] The major accounts of the massacre are Brooks, *The Mountain Meadows Massacre*; Bagley, *Blood of the Prophets*; Denton, *American Massacre*; and Walker, Turley, and Leonard, *Massacre at Mountain Meadows*.

[135] MacKinnon, "'Lonely Bones'"; MacKinnon, *At Sword's Point*, 298–312; Turner, *Brigham Young*, 284–286; Bigler, "The Aiken Party Executions and the Utah War."

effects on groups as well as individuals, especially when they have been victimized precisely because of their group identity. Social psychologist Ervin Staub describes some of the effects of post-traumatic stress on groups. Having been victimized in the past, members of a group may harbor feelings of anxiety, hostility, and anger toward other people. These sentiments can in turn justify the desire to do harm to others before they are able to do harm to you – a kind of inverted Golden Rule. "Unhealed psychological wounds," Staub argues, "can, under certain conditions, lead some former victims to become perpetrators . . . Perceiving a threat, people may engage in what they believe is self-defense – but their 'defensive violence' may be unnecessary or more forceful than necessary." Some people repress or are able to reconcile past victimization. For others, however, "Deep injuries in the past often become a strong part of the individual's and group's identity. The group can define itself, see itself and the world, and interpret new events from the perspective of that past history and its meaning to the group . . . Victimization and trauma can become central to the group's history, identity, and orientation to the world."[136]

In perceiving the marching army as a mob, Latter-day Saint settlers were not suffering from irrational paranoia. They had been the victims of very real atrocities in the years prior to emigrating west, and rather than providing redress to their grievances now the government was marshaling its armed forces to subdue them. But the Saints were not just victims in this drama. They were also historical agents who displaced their traumas and festering antipathies onto parties who had not done them harm and who did not represent an existential threat. The massacre at Mountain Meadows is the most appalling example of this, but it also helps explain other episodes of Mormon violence in that tragic year of 1857. Unintentionally and unwittingly, President Buchanan's decision to send the US army against the Saints stoked in them the embers of their past trauma and helped ignite a conflagration that engulfed scores of "Gentile" innocents who under other circumstances may well have received humane treatment from the Saints. Their own historical experiences as victims of violence provided a powerful script for Latter-day Saints in perpetrating violence against others.

---

[136] Staub, *Overcoming Evil*, 274–277.

"Apostates": Violence against Dissenters and Deviants

Treason – defined in part as giving "aid and comfort" to the nation's enemies – is one of the few crimes enumerated in the US Constitution.[137] The fear of betrayal from within did not originate with the Founding Fathers. The ancient Greek tragedian Aeschylus wrote, "I have learned to hate all traitors; no disease do I spit on more than treachery."[138] In the Book of Mormon, Nephite dissenters are portrayed as far more retrograde than the perpetually and predictably antagonistic Lamanites. Indeed, the turncoat is typically considered to be worse than the enemy: Judas is despised more than Pontius Pilate, Benedict Arnold more than Lord Cornwallis. Traitor, dissenter, apostate, deviant: different shades of infamy, but sharing a common thread of threatening the integrity, harmony, and purity of the community from within. Minority groups are especially sensitive to betrayals, since their existence is already often tenuous and their level of vulnerability high. For many religious enclaves, therefore, "maintaining the cohesion and purity" of the community becomes paramount, "a full-time job" for the faithful.[139]

As anti-Mormon persecution increased, so did the Latter-day Saints' prioritization of maintaining community cohesion. The Saints often blamed their troubles on dissent originating from within the church. Quelling that dissent – usually framed as "apostasy" – occupied much of the time and attention of the movement's leaders, and loyalty became a prime Latter-day Saint virtue. Upon taking leadership of the church, Brigham Young soon let it be known that malcontents were unwelcome in the community and should leave voluntarily or be subject to the Mormons' own brand of vigilantism.[140] Young's invective against dissenters was often biting. In an 1853 sermon he stormed, "Now, you nasty apostates, clear out." After

---

[137] US Constitution, Article III Section 3.

[138] Aeschylus, *Aeschylus I: The Persians, Seven against Thebes, The Suppliant Maidens, Prometheus Bound*, eds. David Greene and Richmond Lattimore, 3rd ed. (Chicago: University of Chicago Press, 2013), 215.

[139] Almond, Appleby, and Sivan, *Strong Religion*, 89.

[140] See Turner, *Brigham Young*, 119–122, 162; Mahas, "'I Intend to Get Up a Whistling School.'"

rehearsing a violent dream in which he saw himself cut the throats of two apostates "from ear to ear," he declared to the congregation, "I say, rather than that apostates should flourish here, I will unsheathe my bowie knife, and conquer or die."[141] But Young could also adopt a gentler approach. In 1856, responding to reports that many disenchanted Saints were planning to leave Utah Territory, Young offered encouragement: "I wish every one to go who prefers doing so, and if they will go like gentlemen, they go with my best feelings."[142] Whether his tongue was covered in honey or vinegar, Young's emphasis on the necessity of internal unity, and the menace of those who threatened it, remained constant.

Unlike his tirades against the federal government and the nation, which he had no actual power over, Young's harangues against so-called apostates did have real effects. For instance, in the church's April 1854 General Conference, he stood before the congregation and denounced Jesse Hartley as "a vagrant, a thief, and a robber." Young thundered in front of the gathered faithful that Hartley "ought to be baptized in Salt Lake with stones tied to him and hold him under 24 hours to wash away the one hundredth part of his sins." This verbal onslaught must have caught anyone who attended the whole conference by surprise, since just the previous day Young had called Hartley on a mission to Texas – normally a sign of the church's favor. Now, however, the church president proclaimed from the pulpit that Hartley should "be sent to hell . . . to preach to the damned," and moved that he be excommunicated on the spot.[143] Hartley had previously been accused (and acquitted) of horse thievery, a capital offense in nineteenth-century America. And Young may have known that Hartley had written a letter to Secretary of War Jefferson Davis recommending that the Latter-day Saint prophet be removed and replaced as territorial governor – an act that in the early Utah theocracy could be taken as both

---

[141] Brigham Young, "Joseph, a True Prophet," *Journal of Discourses* 1:83.

[142] Brigham Young, "The Holy Ghost Necessary in Preaching," *Journal of Discourses* 4:31–32.

[143] Richard S. Van Wagonen, ed., *The Complete Discourses of Brigham Young* (Salt Lake City: Smith-Petit Foundation, 2009), 2:779–780.

treasonous disloyalty and damnable apostasy.[144] Still, the timing and vehemence of Young's denunciation of Hartley remains perplexing.

Whatever sparked Young's outrage, Hartley clearly got the message that his presence had become an offense to the community. Within the month, he started to make his way out of the territory, leaving behind his wife and newborn baby. In the mountains east of Salt Lake City, Hartley ran into a party of men that included Orson Hyde (the president of the church's Quorum of Twelve Apostles), Hosea Stout (a former Danite, Nauvoo Legion commander, and chief of police in Nauvoo), and Bill Hickman (one of Brigham Young's more notorious enforcers). In his memoir, Hickman later wrote that Hyde had given him orders from Young that if they intercepted Hartley they should "have him used up." Hickman obliged, and reported that Hyde affirmed the job was "well done."[145] Available evidence makes it impossible to either prove or disprove Hickman's claim that Young ordered a hit on Hartley and used Hyde to deliver his message. If true, the irony would be tragically rich, since Hyde had temporarily left the church – or "apostatized" – in 1838 when he objected to the vigilante methods employed by the Danites in Missouri.[146]

Most of the violence against dissenters and deviants in early Utah came during a brief but intense period that came to be known as the Mormon Reformation. By the mid-1850s Brigham Young and other church leaders came to believe that the Saints were growing lax in their religious observance and that they could bring about collective spiritual renewal through strenuous, even bellicose, preaching. Mormonism had never before (or since) witnessed the kind of fire-and-brimstone sermons that prevailed in the Reformation of 1856–1857.[147] Even sympathetic observers admitted that the era was characterized by "some fanaticism."[148]

---

[144] See Marquardt, *The Coming Storm.*

[145] Hickman, *Brigham's Destroying Angel*, 97–98, 201–205. See also Brooks, *On the Mormon Frontier*, 2:512, 514.

[146] See Thomas B. Marsh and Orson Hyde, Affidavit, Richmond, Missouri, October 24, 1838, Mormon War Papers, Missouri State Archives.

[147] See Peterson, "The Mormon Reformation of 1856–1857."

[148] Whitney, *History of Utah*, 1:565.

The Reformation's primary purpose was to provoke Latter-day Saints to repentance and conformity. Purity could be achieved through two principal means: voluntary penitence leading to stricter observance of religious norms, or purging the community of apparent spiritual pollutants. In pursuing the latter, church leaders did not mince words. In a sermon entitled "Exposing Wickedness among the Saints," First Presidency member Jedediah Grant declared that "the time has come in which to unsheathe the sword . . . and to cleanse the inside of the platter" – a reference to a Book of Mormon passage in which Captain Moroni suggested using military force to purge the Nephite society of corrupting elements.[149] In an August 1857 sermon on the "limits of forbearance," Heber C. Kimball, another counselor in the First Presidency, reiterated that dissenters' voluntary emigration from the territory "might relieve us from much trouble; for if men turn traitors to God and His servants, their blood will surely be shed, or else they will be damned."[150]

One of the most disturbing elements of the extremism on display during the Mormon Reformation was the teaching of "blood atonement." Brigham Young and other church leaders repeatedly declared that certain sins were so egregious that a guilty person would have to shed his or her own blood in order to be forgiven for their "gross fault" and thereby qualify for salvation in the next life. Young proclaimed that if such transgressors "had their eyes open to see their true condition, they would be perfectly willing to have their blood spilt upon the ground, that the smoke thereof might ascend to heaven as an offering for their sins."[151] Joseph Smith once taught privately that a murderer should have his blood spilled either through shooting or cutting his throat, but Brigham Young and other Reformation-era leaders expanded the list of qualifying sins to include adultery, apostasy,

---

149 Jedediah M. Grant, "Exposing Wickedness among the Saints," *Journal of Discourses* 3:236; see also Alma 60:23–24.

150 Heber C. Kimball, "Limits of Forbearance," *Journal of Discourses* 4:375.

151 Brigham Young, "To Know God Is Eternal Life," *Journal of Discourses* 4:219; Brigham Young, "The People of God Disciplined by Trials," *Journal of Discourses* 4:53.

counterfeiting, theft, and interracial sex.[152] Historical evidence indicating that blood atonement sermons resulted in actual violence is circumstantial and involves only a small handful of cases.[153] In general, blood atonement preaching did not bear much fruit. Most church members shrugged off the proclaimed doctrine, and it never became a core element of Latter-day Saint belief or practice. Either lay members understood their leaders' violent talk to be mere bombast or their own moral sensibilities led them to reject blood atonement as an acceptable practice regardless of what their prophets taught.

What the emotionally and religiously charged climate of the Mormon Reformation did produce was a greater tolerance for the use of vigilante violence to enforce conformity and either intimidate or punish dissidents and deviants.[154] In mid-February 1857, unidentified assailants ambushed John Tobin and three traveling companions while they camped on the banks of the Santa Clara River in southern Utah, leaving three of the four men with nonfatal gunshot wounds. Tobin was a recent convert to the church who was traveling to California to join the army. For much of his journey through central and southern Utah Tobin had been traveling with two released convicts named John Ambrose and Thomas Betts, but the party had split up, as often happened on the trail. In a February 6 letter to local church leaders in the region, Brigham Young instructed that the pair of felons, whom he never named, be closely watched, and perhaps even killed: "Be on the look out now, & have a few trusty men ready in case of need to pursue, retake & punish. We do not suppose there would be any prosecutions for false imprisonments, or tale bearers for witnesses."[155] It seems that

---

[152] Andrew H. Hedges, Alex D. Smith, and Richard Lloyd Anderson, eds., *The Joseph Smith Papers: Journals, Volume 2: December 1841–April 1843* (Salt Lake City: The Church Historian's Press, 2011), 295; Quinn, *The Mormon Hierarchy: Extensions of Power*, 246.

[153] See Peterson, "The Mormon Reformation," 67; Quinn, *The Mormon Hierarchy: Extensions of Power*, 249; Turner, *Brigham Young*, 258.

[154] See Walker, Turley, and Leonard, *Massacre at Mountain Meadows*, 25.

[155] Brigham Young to Bishops & Presidents South, February 6, 1857, Brigham Young Letterpress Copybook, Vol. 3, p. 387, Church History Library, The Church of Jesus Christ of Latter-day Saints, Salt Lake City, Utah.

Tobin and his traveling companions were either confused by their assailants for Ambrose and Betts, or it was believed that the convicts were still in camp with Tobin. In either case, Young's directions to his subordinates in the southern settlements seem to have precipitated the attack on the Tobin party.[156]

The botched ambush on the Santa Clara River fortunately led to no fatalities. But the incident had ripple effects. Young's letters authorizing surveillance and perhaps punitive measures against Ambrose and Betts also contributed, unintentionally, to the murder of three men in Springville, nearly three hundred miles to the north of where the Tobin party was attacked. Having lost his faith in the church, Springville resident William Parrish was preparing to leave Utah Territory. Springville bishop Aaron Johnson got wind of Parrish's plans, and apparently interpreted Young's cryptic instructions in his February 6 letter as a more general endorsement of decisive action against perceived enemies. After consulting with a church council, Johnson sent spies to monitor the "apostate" Parrish and lead him into a trap. One spy, Gardiner "Duff" Potter, convinced Parrish to walk with him at night to a prearranged location, but the operation was bungled when the designated shooter mistook the two men and fatally shot Potter. Upon realizing his error, the assailant tackled Parrish and repeatedly stabbed him, then slit his throat. Separately, another spy accompanied Parrish's son William Jr. to a predetermined spot where the younger Parrish was shot and killed. A second Parrish son, Orrin, was apprehended but released unharmed the next day. No one was ever convicted for the three deaths, and Bishop Johnson was never disciplined for his role in helping orchestrate the murders of three of his flock.[157]

Other graphic instances of violence occurred in Utah as part of a broader pattern of using violence to punish deviance within the community. Manti resident Thomas Lewis had been sentenced to five years' imprisonment for attempted murder. While being escorted to the territorial prison in October 1856, a party of men abducted Lewis, brutally castrated him, and

---

[156] Parshall, "'Pursue, Retake & Punish'"; see also MacKinnon, "'Lonely Bones,'" 141–142.

[157] See Aird, "'You Nasty Apostates, Clear Out.'"

left him for dead bleeding in the snow. Brigham Young refused to condemn Bishop Warren Snow, who had authorized the castration, and defended the action when Lewis's mother complained to him about it.[158] The following year, a bishop in Payson led several members of his ward in fatally shooting a young Latter-day Saint man and his mother for incest. The vigilantes then killed the infant girl born of this incestuous relationship.[159] Violent policing of sexual norms remained common in Utah for the next several decades, paralleling similar actions taken across the nation in the name of protecting male honor, female virtue, and racial purity.[160]

To be clear, most dissidents in nineteenth-century Utah were never violently accosted, and most of those guilty of various perceived sexual transgressions received punishments far short of castration and murder. Vigilante violence was not the normal vehicle for the enforcement of social norms in pioneer Utah, even during the heat of the Reformation. Yet the cases that did occur nevertheless reveal that at least some significant elements of the Latter-day Saint leadership and their deputies, on both a general and local level, had come to accept deadly violence as an effective, if selectively employed, instrument to enforce both their own authority and the people's conformity, all in the name of building a godly society.

In some respects, Latter-day Saint violence in pioneer Utah aligned broadly with many of the contemporaneous patterns of American vigilantism. Even the fact that religious leaders organized and often perpetrated acts of extralegal violence was not atypical for the period.[161] Yet the Saints' violence departed from the norms of nineteenth-century frontier vigilantism on at least two counts. First, some cases, for instance the Hartley and Parrish-Potter murders, took the form of targeted assassinations committed by individual assailants. Summary executions by lone gunmen such as Bill Hickman were not uncommon in the West, but they did not fit the criteria

---

[158] Turner, *Brigham Young*, 258–259.

[159] Quinn, *The Mormon Hierarchy: Extensions of Power*, 253.

[160] See Cannon, "'Mountain Common Law'"; "The Killing of Thos. Coleman Monday Night," *Daily Union Vedette* (Salt Lake City, UT), December 15, 1866. For the national context, see Ireland, "The Libertine Must Die."

[161] See Mason, *The Mormon Menace*, 39–40, 53–54, 165–167.

of "respectable" frontier justice. Second, nineteenth-century Americans accepted vigilantism, insofar as they did, because it met an otherwise unfulfilled need of providing law and order in settings where the foundations of a stable society were not fully established or functional.[162] Pioneer Utah, however, was hardly a typical frontier community. Indeed, the success of Mormon pioneering in the Great Basin was primarily a result of the remarkable solidarity and orderliness provided by the church structure. The Saints' settlements possessed a functioning legal system from the outset, often mediated through the local bishop. The relative effectiveness of Latter-day Saint law enforcement helps explain why Utah was distinctive among states and territories in the American West in that it was the home to almost no large-scale organized vigilantism.[163] In short, Latter-day Saint communities featured mechanisms of social order that could rival long-established cities and towns in the East, thus minimizing if not eliminating the stated purpose of extralegal violence in maintaining social stability.

Much of the violence against dissenters and deviants in pioneer Utah is therefore better categorized as illegal rather than extralegal. That perpetrators were rarely tried let alone convicted of their crimes demonstrates the failure of both the Mormon-controlled justice system in the territory and a clear system of checks and balances on the Latter-day Saint ecclesiastical elite. The resort to extrajudicial means of discipline and punishment undermined the rule of law and eroded moral authority. While in some cases the Saints were acting just like their contemporaries in using violence against unwanted elements in their communities, in other instances they stretched the already elastic norms of the nineteenth-century American frontier.

Particularly during the first decade of the Latter-day Saints' settlement in the Great Basin, they employed violent means in asserting their religious and cultural dominance over the region. Traumatized by multiple bouts of persecution and dispossession, the Saints determined not to let anyone – whether dissidents, Indians, non-Mormon emigrants, or even the US Army – threaten their existence and drive them out again. But just as it had with the Danites in 1838, self-defense quickly morphed into more

---

[162] Brown, *Strain of Violence*, 96–97.
[163] Ibid., 101; Thomas, "Violence across the Land."

assertive and repressive violence, this time against a wider array of enemies. Latter-day Saint violence reached its climax – or nadir – in 1857, then tapered off quickly. Once the embers of the Mormon Reformation had cooled, the Utah War had been resolved peacefully (with the army permanently ensconced outside Salt Lake City), most Indians had been removed from areas of white settlement, and the horror of the Mountain Meadows Massacre became known to at least some in the church leadership, the appetite for using violence as a legitimate method of building the kingdom of God seems to have waned. Out of both principle and pragmatism, the next generation of Latter-day Saint leadership undertook the project of renouncing the violence that their forebears had selectively embraced and replacing it with violence of a different kind.

4 "We Believe in Being Subject": Modernization and State Violence

Shortly after the end of World War I, German sociologist Max Weber argued that in modern times "the relation between the state and violence is an especially intimate one." Weber defined the state as "a human community that (successfully) claims the *monopoly of the legitimate use of physical force* within a given territory." In other words, citizens and nonstate institutions may employ violence only insofar as the state allows it. The properly constituted modern state is therefore the sole arbiter of "legitimate" violence within its borders.[164]

For much of world history, religion was a perfectly legitimate rationale for public violence. That began to change in early modern Europe, when the 1648 Peace of Westphalia put an end to the "wars of religion." Westphalia established the system of sovereign nation-states that has dominated modern international relations, and it did so in part by denying that religion was a good reason for a state to go to war. Over time, religion's authority was differentiated from the state's and relegated to the private realm – a long and complicated process called secularization.[165] An inherent feature of secular

---

[164] Weber, *Politics as a Vocation*, 1–2, emphasis in original.
[165] See Casanova, *Public Religions in the Modern World*; Taylor, *A Secular Age*.

modernity, at least as it has developed in the West, is a public–private divide that places religion firmly in the private sphere and denies it access to the kinds of public authority, including the use of violence, monopolized by the state.

As we have seen, in the first several decades of their history Latter-day Saints did not comply with either a Westphalian or Weberian model of the state. Like other nineteenth-century Americans, the Saints often perceived formal state authority to be either inadequate or unjust, so they sometimes turned to extralegal violence to accomplish their goals. But a series of official determinations and transitions from 1889 to 1898 resulted in the Church of Jesus Christ of Latter-day Saints renouncing any claim on violence, abandoning theocratic politics, and demonstrating loyalty to the nation-state by actively participating in its wars. Theologian William Cavanaugh provocatively argues that we can determine a person's or group's ultimate loyalty by asking not what they are willing to die for, but what they are willing to kill for.[166] In at least this sense, the modern church has been characterized by transference of ultimate loyalty from the kingdom of God to the nation-state. Latter-day Saints entered modernity in no small part by accepting, participating in, and even sanctifying the violence of the state.

Ever since Latter-day Saints started participating in the nation's wars with the full approbation of the church leadership, however, there have been some within the tradition who questioned whether going to war was the best way for the Saints to fulfill the Christian obligation to love their enemies. While the legitimacy of state violence remains an unassailable assumption for most of the Latter-day Saint faithful, these alternative voices for peace reveal the ambivalence toward violence that runs through Mormon scripture, history, theology, and culture.

The End of Mormon Violence

One of the most significant moments in Mormon history came in 1890, when Wilford Woodruff, president of the Church of Jesus Christ of Latter-day Saints, issued a proclamation, called the Manifesto, declaring that the

---

[166] See Cavanaugh, *The Myth of Religious Violence*, 56.

church would conform to "the law of the land" by no longer practicing plural marriage.[167] Less well known, but arguably just as important, was the official declaration issued some nine months earlier under the joint signatures of the First Presidency and Twelve Apostles. In their December 1889 statement, the hierarchy affirmed that "this Church views the shedding of human blood with the utmost abhorrence." They disavowed reports that Mormon apostates had been killed in Utah, arguing (falsely) that "no case of this kind has ever occurred." The leadership denied the doctrine of blood atonement (without naming it), and forcefully denounced as "entirely untrue" the claim that the church "favors or believes in the killing of persons who leave the Church or apostatize from its doctrines." Such an act, they asserted, "is abhorrent to us and is in direct opposition to the fundamental principles of our creed." The only time that a person's blood could be lawfully shed was when the state issued the death penalty for a convicted criminal in a capital case.[168]

Though a little shaky in its rendering of Mormon history, the 1889 official declaration stated unequivocally that the church made no claim on the right to violence, ceding that prerogative entirely to the state. In doing so, church leaders were reaching back to ideas articulated in a declaration on government penned in 1835 by Oliver Cowdery, then serving as Assistant President of the church. Accepted by a general assembly of the church, Cowdery's declaration was canonized in the first edition of the Doctrine and Covenants and remains part of Latter-day Saint scripture today. The 1835 document was comfortably grounded in the broad mainstream of antebellum American political and religious thought. It made a clear distinction between "human laws" that would govern "individuals and nations," and "divine laws" with authority over "faith and worship." Acknowledging the right of secular governments to punish individuals who disturbed the public order, the declaration dismissed any theocratic notions by asserting that "we do not believe it just to mingle religious influence with civil government." Religious institutions had the right to discipline and even excommunicate

---

[167] Doctrine and Covenants, Official Declaration – 1.

[168] Official Declaration, December 12, 1889, in Clark, *Messages of the First Presidency*, 3:184–187. See also Alexander, *Things in Heaven and Earth*, 259.

their members for matters of internal doctrine and polity, but not to "put them in jeopardy of either life or limb, or to inflict any physical punishment upon them."[169] Later developments in the 1840s and 1850s, when the Latter-day Saints did seek to establish a theocracy and employed violence against both internal and external opponents, contradicted the spirit and substance of the 1835 declaration. The church's 1889 declaration therefore leapfrogged several decades of history in order to return the Latter-day Saints to the position they had taken in the early years of the movement.

The significance of the 1889 statement's rejection of theocracy and embrace of state sovereignty cannot be minimized. In 1844 Brigham Young insisted that "No line can be drawn between the church and other governments, of the spiritual and temporal affairs of the church."[170] Yet forty-five years later his successors proclaimed that "Church government and civil government are distinct and separate in our theory and practice, and we regard it as part of our destiny to aid in the maintenance and perpetuity of the institutions of our country."[171] Having once endeavored to leave behind the United States entirely and establish a theocratic kingdom in the West, now Latter-day Saint prophets and apostles taught that promoting the "perpetuity" of the secular nation-state was an essential part of the church's "destiny." Fully acceding to the state's sovereignty necessarily meant acknowledging its monopoly on violence. The 1889 declaration marked the end of any Latter-day Saint claim that violence could be a legitimate instrument to advance the church and kingdom of God – a disavowal that has not been questioned since.

The Acceptance of State Violence

Beginning in the 1890s, and proceeding in fits and starts, Latter-day Saint leadership charted a new course for the church predicated upon its capitulation to secular authority. The notion of Zion now expanded to encompass the nation-state. As scholar Ethan Yorgason observed, "Americanization

---

[169] Doctrine and Covenants 134:6, 8–10, 12.

[170] Grow, *Council of Fifty, Minutes*, 82.

[171] Clark, *Messages of the First Presidency*, 3:186–187.

implied transfer of Mormons' political obedience from one institution to another: from the church to the nation and its political system."[172]

A major feature of modern nationalism is that citizens are expected to participate in, or at least support, the nation's wars. Until the 1890s, however, the Saints' relationship to the United States' wars was decidedly ambivalent. When war broke out with Mexico in 1846, US army officers visited the Mormon pioneers' camp in Iowa and requested five hundred volunteers. It was an awkward proposal, since the Saints were in the process of leaving the nation they believed had turned its back on them and failed to protect their basic liberties. Nevertheless, Brigham Young saw the offer as an opportunity, even an act of providence, whereby the Saints could get money (and guns) from the government that would assist in their transcontinental migration. Thus was formed the Mormon Battalion, which embarked on a historic 2,000-mile march that ultimately helped secure California as a territory of the United States, all without ever engaging Mexican troops in battle. As historian Ronald Walker suggests, Latter-day Saint participation in the Mexican-American War is best understood as a self-interested action that drew upon abstract loyalty to the American nation more than a particular yearning for war.[173]

When the American Civil War came, the Saints stayed on the sidelines, nursing their grievances against the federal government and harboring dark apocalyptic fantasies. At least four factors combined to prevent the Saints from rushing to join the Union's ranks. First, the Saints enjoyed the luxury of geographic isolation in Utah. Second, the firing on Fort Sumter occurred only three years after the conclusion of the Utah War, and the Saints were hardly in the mood to join the nation's army that had just marshaled its forces against them. Third, in their quest to protect their right to practice plural marriage, Latter-day Saint had found Democrats from the South to be political allies due to their shared commitment to local rule and popular sovereignty. Fourth, the Mormon Reformation and Utah War inspired a new wave of Mormon millennialism. Believing the return of Christ was

---

[172] Yorgason, *Transformation of the Mormon Culture Region*, 149; see all of chap. 4. See also Alexander, *Mormonism in Transition*, chap. 2.

[173] Walker, "Sheaves, Bucklers, and the State," 273–274.

near, Latter-day Saints disengaged from the surrounding society. They saw the war between the states as the literal fulfillment of an 1832 prophecy by Joseph Smith that predicted that "war will be poured out upon all nations ... beginning at the rebellion of South Carolina, which will eventually terminate in the death and misery of many souls ... For behold, the Southern States shall be divided against the Northern States," and "slaves shall rise up against their masters, who shall be marshaled and disciplined for war." In the midst of this terrible conflict the Saints were counseled to "stand ye in holy places, and be not moved, until the day of the Lord come; for behold, it cometh quickly."[174] Smarting from persecution, some of the Saints actually delighted in reading reports of the war's horrific bloodshed, believing the nation was finally reaping what it had sown. Though a few church members did enlist, and Utah remained loyal to the Union, the Saints were mostly content to sit out the prophesied war in which "the wicked would slay the wicked."[175]

The conflict between Latter-day Saints and the United States reached a boiling point in the quarter century after Appomattox. In what was known as "the Raid," federal marshals roamed Utah Territory to arrest polygamists, and much of the church leadership spent the 1880s either in prison or in hiding. Though the threat of mass violence never presented itself as it had during the Utah War, a concerted campaign undertaken by all three branches of the federal government to suppress the church's theocracy and polygamy was complemented by hundreds of local acts of vigilante violence against Latter-day Saints particularly in the American South.[176] The church leadership's official declarations of 1889 and 1890 therefore represented both pragmatism and exhaustion. The ensuing rapprochement between the Latter-day Saints and the US government culminated in Utah finally being granted statehood in 1896.

In the wake of statehood, grateful church leaders were eager to display their loyalty to the nation, and the McKinley administration's manufactured war against Spain in 1898 gave them a perfect chance to do so. Latter-day

---

[174] Doctrine and Covenants 87:1–4, 6, 8.

[175] George A. Smith, "Variety of Gifts," *Journal of Discourses* 9:348.

[176] See Gordon, *The Mormon Question*; Mason, *The Mormon Menace*.

Saints' opinions about the escalating conflict were divided until President McKinley formally declared war, at which point most church leaders got in line behind the commander-in-chief. The main holdout was apostle Brigham Young Jr., son of the famous pioneer leader, who was not a pacifist but believed this particular war was a fundamentally "unrighteous cause."[177] In a council of church leaders in late April 1898, George Q. Cannon, a member of the First Presidency who had also served as Utah's territorial representative to Congress for many years, argued that "Our young men might distinguish themselves in this war," whereupon Young saucily countered, "Yes, they would undoubtedly extinguish themselves." If any young Latter-day Saint man was itching to serve in a great cause, Young said he should go "on a mission to preach the gospel of peace." The day after President McKinley called for volunteers, Young delivered a sermon in the Salt Lake Tabernacle in which he insisted, "There are other ways in which we can show our patriotism than by sending our sons to fight for our country at this crisis." Concerned at the prospect of losing the nation's favor, the First Presidency immediately published an editorial entitled "No Disloyalty Here" and ordered Young to cease his public protests. The apostle publicly obeyed the gag order but maintained his disgust with the war in his private diary.[178] In the end, Utah quickly filled its initial quota of five hundred volunteers, who were greeted with cheering crowds as they left Salt Lake City. Some of them received special blessings of protection in the Salt Lake Temple.[179] Not all of the Saints came marching home from Secretary of State John Hay's "splendid little war"; three of Young's own cousins were killed in the conflict.

This willingness of Latter-day Saints to fight for the US government – as opposed to simply taking its money and guns as the Mormon Battalion did five decades earlier – marked a significant turning point in Mormon history. The 1889 official declaration disclaimed violence as a legitimate expression of the Latter-day Saints' religion, but it was silent on the question of war. Only nine years later, the church's prophets and apostles, save one,

---

[177] Quoted in Walker, "Sheaves, Bucklers, and the State," 277.

[178] Quinn, "The Mormon Church and the Spanish-American War," 361–363.

[179] Walker, "Sheaves, Bucklers, and the State," 278.

encouraged the youth of Zion to "distinguish themselves" by killing for their country. This constituted a fundamental reordering of the Mormon worldview. As historian Michael Quinn concluded, "After 1898 ... the Mormon church, recognizing national authority as supreme, would no longer claim the right to determine when and where Mormons would fight and die."[180] One of nineteenth-century America's most robust alternative polities, the Mormon kingdom in the West, entirely ceded its temporal sovereignty, including the right to violence, to the state. It was a triumph of modern statebuilding.

Modern War

Since the Spanish-American War, every time the nation has called for Latter-day Saint citizens to die and kill on its behalf the church and its members have responded affirmatively. A consistent pattern emerged throughout the twentieth century: Latter-day Saint leaders were against war until the government entered one, at which point they encouraged military service as a duty of the faithful. World War I was a good test case, because the war commenced in Europe and had proven its devastating results long before Americans entered the conflict. In his opening address to the church's October 1914 General Conference, held some two and a half months after Europe had become engulfed in war, church president and prophet Joseph F. Smith spoke eloquently against militarism. In rehearsing the carnage brought by the war, President Smith insisted, "God did not design or cause this. It is deplorable to the heavens that such a condition should exist among men."[181] Under Smith's direction, his counselor Charles W. Penrose offered a formal prayer for peace in which he petitioned that God would "prepare the way whereby war may cease and peace may be established." The Latter-day Saints "desire to be ambassadors of peace," Penrose affirmed.[182]

---

[180] Quinn, "The Mormon Church and the Spanish-American War," 366.

[181] Joseph F. Smith, "Opening Address," *Eighty-Fifth Semi-Annual Conference of the Church of Jesus Christ of Latter-day Saints* (Salt Lake City: Deseret News, 1914), 7.

[182] Charles W. Penrose, "A Prayer for Peace," *Eighty-Fifth Semi-Annual Conference*, 9.

By April 1917, when the US Congress voted to declare war on Germany, Penrose was no longer praying for peace. "True, Jesus Christ taught that non-resistance was right and praiseworthy and a duty under certain circumstances and conditions," he preached. But "Jesus was no milksop," and he didn't expect his people to lie down and be slaughtered. Furthermore, it was the duty of the Latter-day Saints to defend "the rights of the nation of which we form a part." Citing various passages from the Doctrine and Covenants, Penrose concluded, "Does the Lord permit the shedding of blood and justify it? Yes, sometimes he does."[183] President Joseph F. Smith, who had so ardently spoken against the war, now walked a fine line. He taught that even when "brought into action with the enemy," Latter-day Saint soldiers were called to "maintain above all other things the spirit of humanity, of love, and of peace-making." He implored church members to keep in mind the seeming paradox that "when they become soldiers of the State and of the Nation ... they will not forget that they are also soldiers of the Cross, that they are ministers of life and not of death." Though decidedly more ambivalent than his counselor Penrose, President Smith ultimately arrived at a similar conclusion that the Saints shared in the "grand and necessary duty of protecting and guarding our Nation from the encroachments of wicked enemies, cruel and destructive foes."[184]

Due to the church's success in global evangelism, in 1917 there were also Latter-day Saints in the Central Powers who felt equally patriotic about serving the nations that their American prophet had labeled as "wicked enemies, cruel and destructive foes." Approximately five hundred Latter-day Saints enlisted for Germany at the war's outset, and about seventy-five Saints died fighting for the Kaiser.[185] World War I was thus the first time in which members of the Church of Jesus Christ of Latter-day Saints participated broadly on both sides of an international conflict. Virtually at war

---

[183] Charles W. Penrose, untitled remarks, *Eighty-Seventh Annual Conference of the Church of Jesus Christ of Latter-day Saints* (Salt Lake City: Deseret News, 1917), 19–21.

[184] Joseph F. Smith, untitled remarks, *Eighty-Seventh Annual Conference*, 3–4.

[185] Hyrum W. Valentine, untitled remarks, *Eighty-Seventh Annual Conference*, 148; Walker, "Sheaves, Bucklers, and the State," 281, 298 n. 82.

with the American nation only a generation earlier, now Latter-day Saints fought one another in a world war at the behest of their respective nations.

A similar pattern held true in World War II, with Latter-day Saints rallying to their respective flags. Most German Saints supported the Third Reich, and church leaders developed a coordinated approach to not only avoid trouble but also curry favor with Hitler's regime.[186] Individual Saints who resisted the Nazi government did so with no ecclesiastical support, and the church quickly disavowed such acts. For instance, Helmuth Hübener, beheaded in a Gestapo prison at the age of 17 for the distribution of anti-Nazi propaganda, was excommunicated by local church leaders; they posthumously reinstated his church membership only after the war's end.[187]

The dilemmas posed by World War II prompted the church's First Presidency to issue its most important and detailed statement regarding war. These leaders affirmed their commitment to the duties of national citizenship, as expressed in one of the church's thirteen Articles of Faith: "We believe in being subject to kings, presidents, rulers, and magistrates, in obeying, honoring, and sustaining the law." Walking a theological and political tightrope, the First Presidency denounced war while supporting church members' participation in it:

> The Lord is a Lord of peace. He has said to us in this dispensation: "Therefore, renounce war and proclaim peace . . . "
>
> Thus, the Church is and must be against war. The Church itself cannot wage war, unless and until the Lord shall issue new commands. It cannot regard war as a righteous means of settling international disputes; these should and could be settled – the nations agreeing – by peaceful negotiation and adjustment.
>
> But the Church membership are citizens or subjects of sovereignties over which the Church has no control . . . When, therefore, constitutional law, obedient to these

[186] See Nelson, *Moroni and the Swastika*.
[187] See Holmes and Keele, *When Truth Was Treason*.

principles, calls the manhood of the Church into the armed
service of any country to which they owe allegiance, their
highest civic duty requires that they meet that call.

In short, the First Presidency made the distinction that the church could
never itself be party to armed conflict, but its members were not only
encouraged but duty-bound to demonstrate their civic loyalty by participating in the nation's wars. To assuage the consciences of Latter-day Saints
who had been taught not to kill, the leadership taught that any moral guilt
associated with a soldier taking another person's life in the course of his
duty would be imputed by God toward the political leaders who led the
nation into war. With echoes of Abraham Lincoln's Second Inaugural
Address, the church leadership acknowledged the moral complexities atten-
dant to being a global body in the midst of a world war: "[The church's]
devoted members are in both camps . . . On each side they believe they are
fighting for home and country and freedom. On each side, our brethren
pray to the same God, in the same name, for victory. Both sides cannot be
wholly right; perhaps neither is without wrong."[188] No statement more
fully captures the ambivalence of the sacred.

The twentieth-century Latter-day Saint embrace of the sacred duty to
participate in state violence, regardless of the relative virtues of the government or its wars, became so deeply engrained that church leaders openly
denounced conscientious objectors during the Vietnam War. This represented yet another departure from earlier teaching and practice. During the
Civil War, Brigham Young praised the "peaceably disposed" men fleeing to
the West to escape enlistment, saying, "I think they are probably as good
a class of men as has ever passed through this country; they are persons who
wish to live in peace . . . I have no fault to find with them."[189] Decades later,
at the end of World War II, the church-owned *Deseret News* published an
editorial praising "the earnest, sincere, loyal conscientious objector, who,

---

[188] "Message of the First Presidency," *One Hundred Twelfth Annual Conference of the
Church of Jesus Christ of Latter-day Saints* (Salt Lake City: The Church of Jesus
Christ of Latter-day Saints, 1942), 88–97.

[189] Brigham Young, "Necessity for Watchfulness," *Journal of Discourses* 10:248.

because of his religious convictions, asked to be relieved of military service which would necessitate his taking the life of a fellowman."[190] Latter-day Saints even had their own tradition of civil disobedience in the form of a decades-long campaign of nonviolent resistance to the federal government's antipolygamy efforts.[191]

Church leaders in the Vietnam period departed from these precedents and doubled down on the sacred duty of state violence. In a typical statement, apostle Boyd K. Packer told the church in 1968, "Though all the issues of the conflict [in Vietnam] are anything but clear, the matter of citizenship responsibility is perfectly clear."[192] In response to individual church members seeking advice or the church's blessing for receiving conscientious objector (CO) status during the increasingly unpopular war, the First Presidency insisted that "membership in the Church of Jesus Christ of Latter-day Saints does not make one a conscientious objector." In applying for CO status a man might appeal to his own interpretation of church doctrines, but he could not simply cite his membership in the church as evidence for his pacifism.[193]

Little changed as the church encountered the complex geopolitical landscape of the twenty-first century. In the October 2001 General Conference, held less than a month after the September 11 terrorist attacks, church Prophet-President Gordon B. Hinckley echoed his predecessors while reflecting on the brewing "war on terror." "We are people of peace," he asserted. "But there are times when we must stand up for right and decency, for freedom, and civilization."[194] A year and a half later, in the midst of the American-led coalition invasion of Iraq, Hinckley spoke again, and in more

---

190 Quoted in Quinn, "Pacifist Counselor in the First Presidency," 152.

191 Pulsipher, "'Prepared to Abide the Penalty.'"

192 Quoted in Walker, "Sheaves, Bucklers, and the State," 286.

193 Letter from Joseph Anderson, Secretary to the First Presidency, to anonymous, March 20, 1970, reprinted in Thomasson, *War, Conscription, Conscience and Mormonism*, 6.

194 Gordon B. Hinckley, "The Times in Which We Live," October 2001 General Conference, available online at www.lds.org/general-conference/2001/10/the-times-in-which-we-live?lang=eng.

detail, on "War and Peace." Aware of critiques of a new American empire, he spoke out against the history of regimes extending their power by means of "brutal conquest, of subjugation, of repression." He conceded the seeming disagreement even within Latter-day Saint scriptures on whether followers of Christ should "renounce war and proclaim peace" or take up weapons in support of their nation. In the end, President Hinckley took a position inspired by his reading of the war chapters in the Book of Mormon. Latter-day Saints are citizens of nations, he said, and "there are times and circumstances when nations are justified, in fact have an obligation, to fight for family, for liberty, and against tyranny, threat, and oppression." God would not hold soldiers accountable for the wartime actions "which they are legally obligated to do," and may even "hold us responsible if we try to impede or hedge up the way of those who are involved in a contest with forces of evil and repression." In supporting the American war effort and leveling a hermeneutic of suspicion toward antiwar protesters, Hinckley made clear that he was expressing his "personal feelings." But his words came in the most authoritative venue possible in the church – the Prophet-President speaking at the pulpit in General Conference. Speaking in harmony with statements of church leaders since 1889, the prophet maintained that in a time of war members of the Church of Jesus Christ of Latter-day Saints, particularly those enlisted in the armed forces, had the paramount obligation "to execute the will of the sovereign."[195]

The Iraq War tested Latter-day Saints' relationship to state violence in ways that went beyond the battlefield. In 2014, a declassified report of the US Senate's Select Committee on Intelligence revealed that two Saints were involved in providing legal justification for the Bush administration's design and implementation of "enhanced interrogation" techniques. One of the two men was shortly thereafter called to be a bishop, the presiding officer in a local Latter-day Saint congregation, but resigned within a week after a public outcry. Many observers pointed out that the actions of two individuals do not speak for their religion or its theology, and there were

---

[195] Gordon B. Hinckley, "War and Peace," April 2003 General Conference, available online at www.lds.org/general-conference/2003/04/war-and-peace?lang=eng.

plenty of Latter-day Saints who were discomfited by the United States' use of torture. Yet when an interfaith group of religious leaders in Utah composed an ecumenical statement in 2005 denouncing the government's use of torture, the Church of Jesus Christ of Latter-day Saints declined to sign on. A spokesman said that the church "condemns inhumane treatment of any person under any circumstances" but "has not taken a position on any proposed legislative or administrative actions regarding torture."[196]

In sum, in the last decade of the nineteenth century Latter-day Saints ceded to the state the authority to justify and perpetrate violence, then spent the twentieth and part of the twenty-first centuries participating in state violence whenever called upon. The church adopted what legal scholar Nathan Oman calls an "apolitical theology of the state," which "emphasized the role of Latter-day Saints as good citizens and sought to reassure often skeptical government officials that the church was uninterested in operating as an agent of radical political or social change."[197] The upshot is that the church has had marvelous success securing entry for its missionaries in countries around the world so that it can advance its mission of preaching the gospel and saving souls. In order to accomplish that mission the church has fully acceded to the sovereignty of the state, which has entailed accepting the state's monopoly on violence and providing what has functionally been rubber stamp approval for the military actions of whatever nation Latter-day Saints find themselves in. Since 1898 Latter-day Saints have fit comfortably into William Cavanaugh's thought experiment: killing in the name of religion is abhorrent and unthinkable, while killing in the name of the state seems to be a perfectly reasonable and even sacred duty.

---

[196] Jana Riess, "Is Mormonism responsible for torture?," *Religion Dispatches*, 10 December 2014, https://religionnews.com/2014/12/10/mormonism-responsible-torture/; David Grant, "Two Mormons Accused in Senate Torture Memos, a Third Praised for Refusing," *Mormon Hub*, December 13, 2014, https://mormonhub.com/blog/buzz/two-mormons-accused-senate-torture-memos-third-praised-refusing/; Carrie A. Moore, "Religions decry use of torture," *Deseret News*, November 24, 2005.

[197] Oman, "International Legal Experience and the Mormon Theology of the State," 29.

Critiquing State Violence

Though pervasive, Latter-day Saints' embrace of state violence has never been absolute. A persistent if often muted tradition of lament and critique appeared throughout the twentieth century. Alternatingly internationalist, isolationist, intellectual, and prophetic in nature, this Latter-day Saint critique of state violence represents an important minority tradition within the tradition that helps provide ballast against the pull of religious nationalism and its uncritical acceptance of state power.

Throughout the first decade of the twentieth century, the Church of Jesus Christ of Latter-day Saints formally sponsored "peace meetings" as a collective witness against the evils of war. Held annually to commemorate the Hague Peace Conference of 1899, which resulted in a series of treaties designed to encourage the peaceful settlement of international disputes, these peace meetings were elaborate affairs typically organized and led by local women. Latter-day Saints decorated their local meetinghouses in preparation for their gatherings, which featured the singing of hymns and antiwar songs, speeches supporting international arbitration, and the formal adoption of peace resolutions. For example, attendees at one peace meeting in 1906 decried "the brutal clash of arms, the useless shedding of blood, and the wanton destruction of human life" and vowed to "be disciples of peace." Despite its sincerity, the international peace movement was unable to prevent the coming of World War I, which in turn brought an end to the peace meetings.[198]

Whereas the peace meetings were motivated by an idealistic internationalism, the pacifist views of prominent mid-twentieth-century church leader J. Reuben Clark were more pessimistic and isolationist in nature. Clark had a distinguished career as an attorney and US ambassador before being called to the church's First Presidency from 1933 to 1961. An ardent supporter of American power earlier in his life, he became increasingly skeptical of militarism in the years after World War I and eventually served on the national board of directors of the American Peace Society. As

[198] David Pulsipher, "When Mormon Women Led Out for Peace," *Juvenile Instructor*, March 20, 2012, http://juvenileinstructor.org/when-mormon-women-led-out-for-peace/. See also Arrington, "Modern Lysistratas."

a counselor to three different church presidents, Clark signed multiple First Presidency statements endorsing the participation of Latter-day Saints in war. His own personal views, however, remained far more critical. In his draft of a First Presidency statement following the Japanese attack on Pearl Harbor, Clark lambasted young Latter-day Saints eager to enlist so as to gain "commissions to kill their fellow men . . . It is not the Master's way. It is the jungle law of the beasts." (Church president Heber J. Grant opted for a revised message that more blandly denounced "cruelty, hate, and murder.")[199] In General Conference a year after the war's end, Clark excoriated the United States' use of the atomic bomb in Hiroshima and Nagasaki, which he characterized as "the crowning savagery of the war." He particularly lamented the fact that the population of the United States, including Latter-day Saints, gave their "general approval of this fiendish butchery."[200] However, Clark's critique of the national war effort was not uncomplicated. Even after learning of some of the horrors of the Nazi regime, a personal anti-Semitic streak informed his isolationist attitudes.[201] The most highly placed pacifist within the church's twentieth-century leadership thus left an ambivalent legacy as a critic of state violence.

Two prominent twentieth-century Latter-day Saint intellectuals also emerged as avowed opponents of war. Hugh Nibley served as an intelligence officer attached for most of World War II to the 101st Airborne division, and came away from the war convinced of its futility and wickedness. A gifted scholar of ancient history and languages who spent decades on the religion faculty of Brigham Young University and became one of the Latter-day Saints' most notable apologists, Nibley peppered his voluminous writings with devastating critiques of war and militarism. As his biographer noted, Nibley's "commitment to pacifism was constant and unwavering."[202] Another popular and longtime BYU professor, Eugene England, also

[199] Quinn, "Pacifist Counselor in the First Presidency," 151–153.

[200] J. Reuben Clark, untitled remarks, in *One Hundred Seventeenth Semi-Annual Conference of the Church of Jesus Christ of Latter-day Saints* (Salt Lake City: The Church of Jesus Christ of Latter-day Saints, 1946), 88.

[201] Quinn, "Pacifist Counselor in the First Presidency," 149 n. 46.

[202] Petersen, "The Work of Death," 166.

consistently advocated for peace in his writings and lectures. While allowing that war could be "justified under certain conditions," England nevertheless embraced a strict peace ethic that ruled out virtually all use of military force, from the war in Vietnam to the first Gulf War. England developed a distinctly Latter-day Saint philosophy of "effective pacifism" in which we "must do, in love, whatever we can that will *genuinely create peace*," even if that action requires us to "sacrifice our lives."[203]

Historical peace meetings, the largely private sentiments of a lone church leader, and the musings of two intellectuals can all be easily brushed aside by Latter-day Saints inclined to support the violence of the state. It is far harder for the faithful to dismiss the public teachings of their prophets, making statements by church presidents George Albert Smith and Spencer W. Kimball particularly significant. In February 1946, the First Presidency under George Albert Smith sent a letter to the congressional delegation from Utah formally opposing a peacetime draft and compulsory military training. In seventeen points, the letter expressed deep concern about what the permanent mobilization of the citizenry would do for their and the nation's character. Universal military service would "teach our sons not only the way to kill but also, in too many cases, the desire to kill," thus leaving them "indoctrinated . . . to believe in the ways of war" rather than peace. Creating a "great war machine" would tempt other nations to do the same, and thus "make of the whole earth one great military camp whose separate armies, headed by war-minded officers, will never rest till they are at one another's throats in what will be the most terrible contest the world has ever seen." The First Presidency concluded by extolling the virtues of diplomacy and asserting, "What this country needs and what the world needs, is a will for peace, not war."[204]

A generation later, the June 1976 issue of the church's official magazine for adults, *Ensign*, was dedicated to celebrating the United States' bicentennial, featuring articles with titles such as "A Promised Land" and

---

[203] Ericson, "Eugene England's Theology of Peace," 173. See also England, *Making Peace*.

[204] Letter of the First Presidency, December 14, 1945, reprinted in *The Improvement Era*, February 1946, 76–77.

"Teaching Patriotism in the Home." Especially within that context, the message and tone of church Prophet-President Spencer W. Kimball's contribution, a jeremiad entitled "The False Gods We Worship," could not have been more jarring. Kimball condemned "the general state of wickedness" in the nation and world, concluding that "we are, on the whole, an idolatrous people – a condition most repugnant to the Lord." After decrying materialism and pride, the prophet turned his withering gaze toward church members' uncritical, "idolatrous" embrace of violence, particularly war. Kimball's message is so penetrating, and so unlike anything else in modern Latter-day Saint discourse, that it is worth quoting at length:

> We are a warlike people, easily distracted from our assignment of preparing for the coming of the Lord. When enemies rise up, we commit vast resources to the fabrication of gods of stone and steel – ships, planes, missiles, fortifications – and depend on them for protection and deliverance. When threatened, we become antienemy instead of pro-kingdom of God; we train a man in the art of war and call him a patriot, thus, in the manner of Satan's counterfeit of true patriotism, perverting the Savior's teaching:

> "Love your enemies, bless them that curse you, do good to them that hate you, and pray for them which despitefully use you, and persecute you; That ye may be the children of your Father which is in heaven."
> (Matt. 5:44–45)

> We forget that if we are righteous the Lord will either not suffer our enemies to come upon us – and this is the special promise to the inhabitants of the land of the Americas – or he will fight our battles for us . . .

> What are we to fear when the Lord is with us? Can we not take the Lord at his word and exercise a particle of faith in him? Our assignment is affirmative: to forsake the things of the world as ends in themselves; to leave off idolatry and

> press forward in faith; to carry the gospel to our enemies, that they might no longer be our enemies.[205]

Kimball applied his own teachings a few years later, when he and his counselors formally opposed President Ronald Reagan's proposal to base the MX missile system in Utah and Nevada.[206]

The First Presidency's 1946 letter and President Kimball's 1976 message stand as the two most direct prophetic indictments of state violence emerging from the modern Church of Jesus Christ of Latter-day Saints. While church presidents' teachings normally enjoy enormous prestige among the faithful, however, these particular statements have largely been neglected by subsequent church leaders and official church publications. Nevertheless, the peace witness of Brigham Young Jr., J. Reuben Clark, Hugh Nibley, Eugene England, George Albert Smith, and Spencer W. Kimball are part of the historical record. Together they help form an authentically Latter-day Saint critique of state-sponsored violence that is available for retrieval and application by church members seeking to deploy the resources of their religious tradition to build a more peaceful world.

In the end, who represents the conscience of the modern church when it comes to state violence? The intellectuals who have interpreted Latter-day Saint scripture and theology to be decidedly antiwar, if not pacifist? The prophets who denounced militarism and equated it with idolatry? The two men who apparently believed they were acting according to both their civic duty and moral compass when they facilitated the state's use of torture? Or the thousands of Latter-day Saints who currently serve in the armed forces of their various nations, buoyed up by official training materials produced

---

[205] Spencer W. Kimball, "The False Gods We Worship," *Ensign*, June 1976, available online at www.lds.org/ensign/1976/06/the-false-gods-we-worship?lang=eng.

[206] First Presidency Statement on Basing of MX Missile, *Ensign*, June 1981, available online at www.lds.org/ensign/1981/06/news-of-the-church/first-presidency-statement-on-basing-of-mx-missile?lang=eng; Hildreth, "The First Presidency Statement on MX in Perspective."

by the church assuaging their pangs of conscience and counseling them to "Let Not Your Heart Be Troubled"?[207]

"Being subject to kings, presidents, rulers, and magistrates, in obeying, honoring, and sustaining the law," as the church's Article of Faith declares, can take many forms. Select voices of critique notwithstanding, modern Latter-day Saints have largely opted for an interpretation that accepts and even privileges the state's right to summon them to violence. The Saints' hearts and souls might be consecrated to the kingdom of God, but their bodies will, when called upon, be offered up on the altar of the nation.

Epilogue: Toward Peace

An Element titled "Mormonism and Violence" comes with a predetermined narrative, and it is not a happy one. The danger of any sustained treatment of "X and violence" is that it inextricably links X *with* violence in the mind of the reader. While I have endeavored to provide an accurate, if brief, portrayal of the role that violence played in the religion founded two centuries ago by Joseph Smith, this Element is most assuredly *not* a full portrayal of the diverse histories, theologies, cultures, and people of Mormonism. At its worst, a book like this can actually be misleading. Even if all the facts are correct, applying the "and violence" filter to one's subject will necessarily highlight certain aspects while entirely obscuring others.

Mormonism is not an essentially violent religion, nor is Islam, Catholicism, Sikhism, or any other. The percentage of Latter-day Saints (or Muslims, or Catholics, or Sikhs) who have assaulted or killed another human being is tiny, and the number of those who have done so citing explicitly religious justifications would be even more minuscule. Far more common would be the person who testifies that the restored

---

[207] *Let Not Your Hearts Be Troubled: A Message of Peace for Latter-day Saints in Military Service*, available online at www.lds.org/callings/military-relations/orga nization-leader-responsibilites?lang=eng#video2. See also Hudson, Jensen, and Kartchner, *A Time of War, a Time of Peace*.

gospel of Jesus Christ has provided her with inner peace and taught her to treat her family, friends, neighbors, and even enemies with tolerance, kindness, and compassion. That is not to deny the very real strain of violence that runs through Latter-day Saint scripture, history, and culture. It is simply to say that violence is a choice, not an inevitability. Mormonism, like every other religious tradition, contains multiple and complex resources – scriptures, histories, myths, social networks, authority structures, and cosmologies – that can be mobilized in the service of either violence or nonviolence. Religion is fundamentally and always an act of interpretation. Individually and collectively, practitioners choose – within a set of social and cultural structures not necessarily of their own making – both the nature of their worship and how it informs their moral-ethical orientation.

Existing alongside its strain of violence is a distinctive and still emergent Mormon tradition of peacebuilding. In recent decades this nonviolent orientation has flourished in Community of Christ, which has adopted peace as a core component of the church's mission. Increasingly, the Church of Jesus Christ of Latter-day Saints has also taken steps toward acknowledging its sometimes-violent past as well as employing its institutional resources in the service of peace. At a ceremony on the 150th anniversary of the Mountain Meadows Massacre, church apostle Henry B. Eyring expressed "profound regret" for the violent behavior of the nineteenth-century Saints: "What was done here long ago by members of our Church represents a terrible and inexcusable departure from Christian teaching and conduct. We cannot change what happened, but we can remember and honor those who were killed here."[208] In 2014 the Church of Jesus Christ of Latter-day Saints published an essay on its official website entitled "Peace and Violence among 19th-Century Latter-day Saints," formally admitting that "some Church members participated in deplorable violence against people they perceived to be their enemies." The essay concluded by condemning "violent words

---

[208] Greg Hill, "Expressing regret for 1857 massacre," *Church News*, September 15, 2007; see also Carrie A. Moore, "LDS Church Issue Apology over Mountain Meadows," *Deseret News*, September 12, 2007.

and actions" while affirming the church's enduring "commitment to furthering peace throughout the world."[209] At one of the church's universities,
Brigham Young University-Hawaii, that commitment to furthering peace is
being implemented through a highly successful degree and certificate program in Intercultural Peacebuilding. Inspired by a 1955 pronouncement by
church president David O. McKay that the school would send out women
and men committed to "the establishment of peace internationally," the
program provides theoretical and applied training in conflict resolution,
mediation, reconciliation, community building, and cross-cultural leadership, all grounded in distinctive Latter-day Saint teachings, practices, and
values.[210]

In October 2002, scarcely a year after the 9/11 attacks sparked the beginning of America's ongoing "war on terror," apostle Russell M. Nelson – who
became Prophet-President of the Church of Jesus Christ of Latter-day Saints
in January 2018 – delivered a General Conference address entitled "Blessed
Are the Peacemakers." "Because of the long history of hostility upon the
earth," Nelson observed, "many feel that peace is beyond hope." But, he
countered, "I disagree. Peace is possible." Nelson called on Latter-day Saints
and all people of goodwill "to emerge as peacemakers" and to "direct their
powerful potential toward peace." Such peacemakers "could lead in the art of
arbitration, give relief to the needy, and bring hope to those who fear." These
would be the true "patriots" of whom "future generations would shout
praises."[211]

Latter-day Saints earned their stripes as patriots in nations around the
world by fighting in their respective countries' wars. Mormon history and
scriptures are replete with contributions to the long and sad history of

---

[209] "Peace and Violence among 19th-Century Latter-day Saints," available online
at www.lds.org/topics/peace-and-violence-among-19th-century-latter-day-
saints?lang=eng.

[210] See https://davidomckaycenter.byuh.edu/about.

[211] Russell M. Nelson, "Blessed Are the Peacemakers," *Ensign*, November 2002,
39–41, also available online at www.lds.org/general-conference/2002/10/
blessed-are-the-peacemakers?lang=eng.

human violence. But a vision of peace, justice, and healing is also deeply embedded in the heart of the tradition. As the twenty-first-century globe continues to grapple with the dilemmas of violent conflict, so too Mormonism, now approaching its third century, will navigate the complexities of how to pursue peace in a world of violence.

Bibliography

Aird, Polly. "'You Nasty Apostates, Clear Out': Reasons for Disaffection in the Late 1850s." *Journal of Mormon History* 30:2 (Fall 2004): 173–191.

Alexander, Thomas G. *Mormonism in Transition: A History of the Latter-day Saints, 1890–1930.* Urbana: University of Illinois Press, 1986.

Things in Heaven and Earth: The Life and Times of Wilford Woodruff. Salt Lake City: Signature Books, 1993.

Almond, Gabriel A., R. Scott Appleby, and Emmanuel Sivan. *Strong Religion: The Rise of Fundamentalisms around the World.* Chicago: University of Chicago Press, 2003.

Anderson, David, and Andrew Bolton. *Military Service, Pacifism, and Discipleship: A Diversity of Callings?* Independence: Herald Publishing House, 2003.

Anderson, Devery S. *The Development of LDS Temple Worship, 1846–2000.* Salt Lake City: Signature Books, 2011.

Appleby, R. Scott. *The Ambivalence of the Sacred: Religion, Violence, and Reconciliation.* Lanham, MD: Rowman & Littlefield Publishers, 2000.

Arrington, Leonard J. "Modern Lysistratas: Mormon Women in the International Peace Movement, 1899–1939." *Journal of Mormon History* 15 (1989): 89–104.

Bagley, Will. *Blood of the Prophets: Brigham Young and the Massacre at Mountain Meadows.* Norman: University of Oklahoma Press, 2002.

Barlow, Philip L. "To Mend a Fractured Reality: Joseph Smith's Project." *Journal of Mormon History* 38:3 (Summer 2012): 28–50.

Baugh, Alexander L. "A Call to Arms: The 1838 Mormon Defense of Northern Missouri." Ph.D. diss., Brigham Young University, 1996. Reprinted in Dissertations in Latter-day Saint History series. Provo: Joseph Fielding Smith Institute for Latter-day Saint History, 2000.

Bennett, Richard E., Susan Easton Black, and Donald Q. Cannon. *The Nauvoo Legion in Illinois: A History of the Mormon Militia, 1841–1846*. Norman: Arthur H. Clark Co., 2010.

Bigler, David L. "The Aiken Party Executions and the Utah War, 1857–1858." *Western Historical Quarterly* 38:4 (Winter 2007): 457–476.

Blackhawk, Ned. *Violence over the Land: Indians and Empires in the Early American West*. Cambridge: Harvard University Press, 2006.

Bolton, Andrew. "Anabaptism, the Book of Mormon, and the Peace Church Option." *Dialogue: A Journal of Mormon Thought* 37:1 (Spring 2004): 75–94.

Bolton, Andrew, John Hamer, David Howlett, Lachlan Mackay, and Barbara Walden. *In Pursuit of Peace: Community of Christ's Journey*. Independence: Herald Publishing House, 2016.

Book of Doctrine and Covenants. Independence: Herald Publishing House, 2007.

The Book of Mormon: Another Testament of Jesus Christ. Salt Lake City: The Church of Jesus Christ of Latter-day Saints, 1981.

Book of Mormon Student Manual: Religion 121–122. Salt Lake City: The Church of Jesus Christ of Latter-day Saints, 2009.

Bowman, Matthew. *The Mormon People: The Making of an American Faith*. New York: Random House, 2012.

Boyce, Duane. *Even unto Bloodshed: An LDS Perspective on War*. Salt Lake City: Greg Kofford Books, 2015.

Brooks, Juanita. *The Mountain Meadows Massacre*. Stanford: Stanford University Press, 1950.

On the Mormon Frontier: The Diary of Hosea Stout, 1844–1861. 2 vols. Salt Lake City: University of Utah Press and the Utah State Historical Society, 1964.

Brown, Richard Maxwell. *Strain of Violence: Historical Studies of American Violence and Vigilantism*. New York: Oxford University Press, 1975.

Bushman, Richard Lyman. *Joseph Smith: Rough Stone Rolling*. New York: Alfred A. Knopf, 2005.

Cahill, Lisa Sowle. *Love Your Enemies: Discipleship, Pacifism, and Just War Theory*. Minneapolis: Fortress Press, 1994.

Cannon II, Kenneth L. "'Mountain Common Law': The Extralegal Punishment of Seducers in Early Utah." *Utah Historical Quarterly* 51:4 (Fall 1983): 308–327.

Casanova, José. *Public Religions in the Modern World*. Chicago: University of Chicago Press, 1994.

Cavanaugh, William T. *The Myth of Religious Violence: Secular Ideology and the Roots of Modern Conflict*. New York: Oxford University Press, 2009.

Christy, Howard A. "Open Hand and Mailed Fist: Mormon-Indian Relations in Utah, 1847–52." *Utah Historical Quarterly* 46:3 (Summer 1978): 216–235.

Clark, James R., ed. *Messages of the First Presidency of the Church of Jesus Christ of Latter-day Saints, 1833–1964*. 6 vols. Salt Lake City: Bookcraft, 1966.

Cornwall, Rebecca Foster, and Leonard J. Arrington. "Perpetuation of a Myth: Mormon Danites in Five Western Novels, 1840–90." *BYU Studies Quarterly* 23:2 (1983): 147–165.

Corrill, John. *A Brief History of the Church of Christ of Latter Day Saints (Commonly Called Mormons;)*... St. Louis: the author, 1839.

Crawley, Peter, and Richard L. Anderson. "The Political and Social Realities of Zion's Camp." *BYU Studies* 14 (Summer 1974): 406–420.

Daynes, Kathryn M. *More Wives than One: Transformation of the Mormon Marriage System, 1840–1910*. Urbana: University of Illinois Press, 2001.

Deane, Morgan. "Offensive Warfare in the Book of Mormon and a Defense of the Bush Doctrine." In *War and Peace in Our Time: Mormon*

Perspectives, eds. Patrick Q. Mason, J. David Pulsipher, and Richard L. Bushman, 29–39. Salt Lake City: Greg Kofford Books, 2012.

Denton, Sally. *American Massacre: The Tragedy at Mountain Meadows*. New York: Vintage Books, 2004.

The Doctrine and Covenants of the Church of Jesus Christ of Latter-day Saints. Salt Lake City: The Church of Jesus Christ of Latter-day Saints, 1981.

England, Eugene. *Making Peace: Personal Essays*. Salt Lake City: Signature Books, 1995.

Ericson, Loyd. "Eugene England's Theology of Peace." In *War and Peace in Our Times: Mormon Perspectives*, eds. Patrick Q. Mason, J. David Pulsipher, and Richard L. Bushman, 171–188. Salt Lake City: Greg Kofford Books, 2012.

Farmer, Jared. *On Zion's Mount: Mormons, Indians, and the American Landscape*. Cambridge: Harvard University Press, 2008.

Feldberg, Michael. *The Turbulent Era: Riot and Disorder in Jacksonian America*. New York: Oxford University Press, 1980.

Flake, Kathleen. *The Politics of American Religious Identity: The Seating of Reed Smoot, Mormon Apostle*. Chapel Hill: University of North Carolina Press, 2004.

Gentry, Leland Homer, and Todd M. Compton. *Fire and Sword: A History of the Latter-day Saints in Northern Missouri, 1836–1839*. Salt Lake City: Greg Kofford Books, 2010.

Gilje, Paul A. *Rioting in America*. Bloomington: Indiana University Press, 1996.

Givens, Terryl L. *The Book of Mormon: A Very Short Introduction*. New York: Oxford University Press, 2009.

 By the Hand of Mormon: The American Scripture that Launched a New World Religion. New York: Oxford University Press, 2002.

 The Viper on the Hearth: Mormons, Myths, and the Construction of Heresy, updated ed. New York: Oxford University Press, 2013 (1997).

Gordon, Sarah Barringer. *The Mormon Question: Polygamy and Constitutional Conflict in Nineteenth-Century America*. Chapel Hill: University of North Carolina Press, 2002.

Grimsted, David. *American Mobbing, 1828–1861: Toward Civil War*. New York: Oxford University Press, 1998.

"Rioting in its Jacksonian Setting." *American Historical Review* 77 (April 1972): 361–397.

Grow, Matthew J. et al., eds. *Council of Fifty, Minutes, March 1844–January 1846*. Vol. 1 of the Administrative Records series of *The Joseph Smith Papers*, eds. Ronald K. Esplin, Matthew J. Grow, and Matthew C. Godfrey. Salt Lake City: Church Historian's Press, 2016.

Gutjahr, Paul C. *The Book of Mormon: A Biography*. Princeton: Princeton University Press, 2012.

Hallwas, John E. "Mormon Nauvoo from a Non-Mormon Perspective." *Journal of Mormon History* 16 (1990): 53–69.

Hallwas, John E., and Roger D. Launius, eds. *Cultures in Conflict: A Documentary History of the Mormon War in Illinois*. Logan: Utah State University Press, 1995.

Hardy, Grant. *Understanding the Book of Mormon: A Reader's Guide*. New York: Oxford University Press, 2010.

Hickman, Jared. "The *Book of Mormon* as Amerindian Apocalypse." *American Literature* 86:3 (Sept. 2014): 429–461.

Hickman, William Adams and John H. Beadle. *Brigham's Destroying Angel: Being the Life, Confession, and Startling Disclosures of the Notorious Bill Hickman, the Danite Chief of Utah*. Salt Lake City: Shepard Publishing Co., 1904.

Hildreth, Steven A. "The First Presidency Statement on MX in Perspective." *BYU Studies Quarterly* 22:2 (1982): 215–225.

History of the Church of Jesus Christ of Latter-day Saints. 7 vols. 2nd rev. ed. Salt Lake City: Deseret Book Co., 1980.

Holmes, Blair R. and Alan F. Keele, comp., trans., and ed. *When Truth Was Treason: The Story of the Helmuth Hübener Group Based on the Narrative of Karl-Heinz Schnibbe*. Urbana: University of Illinois Press, 1995.

Howlett, David J. and John-Charles Duffy. *Mormonism: The Basics*. New York: Routledge, 2017.

Hudson, Valerie M., Eric Talbot Jensen, and Kerry M. Kartchner, eds. *A Time of War, a Time of Peace: Latter-day Saint Ethics of War and Diplomacy*. Provo: David M. Kennedy Center for International Studies, Brigham Young University, 2017.

Hutchison, William R. *Religious Pluralism in America: The Contentious History of a Founding Ideal*. New Haven: Yale University Press, 2003.

Ireland, Robert M. "The Libertine Must Die: Sexual Dishonor and the Unwritten Law in the Nineteenth-Century United States." *Journal of Social History* 23 (Autumn 1989): 27–44.

Jennings, Warren. "Zion Is Fled: The Expulsion of the Mormons from Jackson County, Missouri." Ph.D. diss., University of Florida, 1962.

Jessee, Dean C. and David J. Whittaker, eds. "The Last Months of Mormonism in Missouri: The Albert Perry Rockwood Journal." *Brigham Young University Studies* 28:1 (Winter 1988): 5–41.

Johnson, Clark V., ed. *Mormon Redress Petitions: Documents of the 1833–1838 Missouri Conflict*. Provo: Religious Studies Center, 1992.

The Joseph Smith Papers. http://josephsmithpapers.org/.

Journal of Discourses. 26 vols. Liverpool and London: [various publishers], 1854–1886.

Juergensmeyer, Mark. *Terror in the Mind of God: The Global Rise of Religious Violence*, 3rd ed., rev. and upd. Berkeley: University of California Press, 2003.

Juergensmeyer, Mark, Margo Kitts, and Michael Jerryson, eds. *The Oxford Handbook of Religion and Violence*. New York: Oxford University Press, 2013.

King Jr., Martin Luther. *I Have a Dream: Writings and Speeches that Changed the World*, ed. James Melvin. Washington, San Francisco: HarperSanFrancisco, 1992.

Krakauer, Jon. *Under the Banner of Heaven: A Story of Violent Faith.* New York: Anchor Books, 2004.

Leonard, Glen M. *Nauvoo: A Place of Peace, a People of Promise.* Salt Lake City: Deseret Book, 2002.

LeSueur, Stephen C. *The 1838 Mormon War in Missouri.* Columbia: University of Missouri Press, 1987.

Liebman, Charles S. "Extremism as a Religious Norm." *Journal for the Scientific Study of Religion* 22:1 (March 1983): 75–86.

Lindell, Jennifer. "Fall from Grace: Mormon Millennialism, Native Americans, and Violence." In *War and Peace in Our Time: Mormon Perspectives*, eds. Patrick Q. Mason, J. David Pulsipher, and Richard L. Bushman, 93–100. Salt Lake City: Greg Kofford Books, 2012.

MacKinnon, William P. *At Sword's Point, Part 1: A Documentary History of the Utah War to 1858.* Norman: Arthur H. Clark Co., 2008.

"'Lonely Bones': Leadership and Utah War Violence." *Journal of Mormon History* 33:1 (Spring 2007): 121–178.

Madson, Joshua. "A Non-Violent Reading of the Book of Mormon." In *War and Peace in Our Time: Mormon Perspectives*, eds. Patrick Q. Mason, J. David Pulsipher, and Richard L. Bushman, 13–28. Salt Lake City: Greg Kofford Books, 2012.

Mahas, Jeffrey David. "'I Intend to Get Up a Whistling School': The Nauvoo Whistling and Whittling Movement, American Vigilante Tradition, and Mormon Theocratic Thought." *Journal of Mormon History* 43:4 (October 2017): 37–67.

Marquardt, H. Michael. *The Coming Storm: The Murder of Jesse Thompson Hartley.* Collector's Edition Keepsake for volume 13 of the Kingdom in the West series, *Playing with Shadows: Voices of Dissent in the*

Mormon West, eds. Polly Aird, Jeff Nichols, and Will Bagley. Norman: Arthur H. Clark Co., 2011.

Mason, Patrick Q. *The Mormon Menace: Violence and Anti-Mormonism in the Antebellum South*. New York: Oxford University Press, 2011.

"Violent and Nonviolent Religious Militancy." In *The Oxford Handbook on Religion, Conflict, and Peacebuilding*, eds. Atalia Omer, R. Scott Appleby, and David Little, 212–235. New York: Oxford University Press, 2015.

"'The Wars and the Perplexities of the Nations': Reflections on Early Mormonism, Violence, and the State." *Journal of Mormon History* 38:3 (Summer 2012): 72–89.

What Is Mormonism? A Student's Introduction. New York: Routledge, 2017.

Mason, Patrick Q., J. David Pulsipher, and Richard L. Bushman, eds. *War and Peace in Our Time: Mormon Perspectives*. Salt Lake City: Greg Kofford Books, 2012.

Mattox, John Mark. "YES—The Book of Mormon as a Touchstone for Evaluating the Theory of Just War." In *Wielding the Sword While Proclaiming Peace: Views from the LDS Community on Reconciling the Demands of National Security with the Imperatives of Revealed Truth*, eds. Valerie M. Hudson and Kerry M. Kartchner, 57–66. Provo: David M. Kennedy Center for International Studies, Brigham Young University, 2004.

Mauss, Armand L. *All Abraham's Children: Changing Mormon Conceptions of Race and Lineage*. Urbana: University of Illinois Press, 2003.

Nelson, David Conley. *Moroni and the Swastika: Mormons in Nazi Germany*. Norman: University of Oklahoma Press, 2015.

Newell, Linda King and Valeen Tippetts Avery. *Mormon Enigma: Emma Hale Smith*, 2nd ed. Urbana: University of Illinois Press, 1994.

Nibley, Hugh. *Since Cumorah*. Vol. 7 in *The Collected Works of Hugh Nibley*, 2nd ed. Salt Lake City: Deseret Book and FARMS, 1988.

"Warfare and the Book of Mormon." In *Brother Brigham Challenges the Saints*, eds. Don E. Norton and Shirley S. Ricks. Salt Lake City: Deseret Book and FARMS, 1994.

Oaks, Dallin H. and Marvin S. Hill. *Carthage Conspiracy: The Trial of the Accused Assassins of Joseph Smith*. Urbana: University of Illinois Press, 1979.

Olmstead, Jacob W. "*A Victim of the Mormons* and *The Danites*: Images and Relics from Early Twentieth-Century Anti-Mormon Silent Films." *Mormon Historical Studies* 5:1 (Spring 2004): 203–221.

Oman, Nathan B. "International Legal Experience and the Mormon Theology of the State, 1945–2012." In *Out of Obscurity: Mormonism since 1945*, eds. Patrick Q. Mason and John G. Turner, 17–36. New York: Oxford University Press, 2016.

Omer, Atalia, R., Scott Appleby, and David Little, eds. *The Oxford Handbook of Religion, Conflict, and Peacebuilding*. New York: Oxford University Press, 2015.

Parshall, Ardis. "'Pursue, Retake & Punish': The 1857 Santa Clara Ambush." *Utah Historical Quarterly* 73:1 (Winter 2005): 64–86.

The Pearl of Great Price. Salt Lake City: The Church of Jesus Christ of Latter-day Saints, 1981.

Pearson, Carol Lynn. "Could Feminism Have Saved the Nephites?" *Sunstone* (March 1996): 32–40.

The Ghost of Eternal Polygamy: Haunting the Hearts and Heaven of Mormon Women and Men. Walnut Creek, CA: Pivot Point Books, 2016.

Petersen, Boyd Jay. "The Work of Death: Hugh Nibley as Scholar, Soldier, Peace Activist." In *War and Peace in Our Time: Mormon Perspectives*, eds. Patrick Q. Mason, J. David Pulsipher, and Richard L. Bushman, 161–170. Salt Lake City: Greg Kofford Books, 2012.

Peterson, Paul. "The Mormon Reformation of 1856–1857: The Rhetoric and the Reality." *Journal of Mormon History* 15 (1989): 59–87.

Pulsipher, J. David. "Buried Swords: The Shifting Interpretive Ground of a Beloved Book of Mormon Narrative." *Journal of Book of Mormon Studies* 26 (2017): 1–47.

"'Prepared to Abide the Penalty': Latter-day Saints and Civil Disobedience." *Journal of Mormon History* 39:3 (Summer 2013): 131–162.

Quinn, D. Michael. "The Culture of Violence in Joseph Smith's Mormonism." *Sunstone* (October 2011): 16–28.

"The Mormon Church and the Spanish-American War: An End to Selective Pacifism." *Pacific Historical Review* 43:3 (Aug. 1974): 342–366.

The Mormon Hierarchy: Extensions of Power. Salt Lake City: Signature Books in association with Smith Research Associates, 1997.

The Mormon Hierarchy: Origins of Power. Salt Lake City: Signature Books in association with Smith Research Associates, 1994.

"Pacifist Counselor in the First Presidency: J. Reuben Clark Jr., 1933–1961." In *War and Peace in Our Time: Mormon Perspectives*, eds. Patrick Q. Mason, J. David Pulsipher, and Richard L. Bushman, 141–160. Salt Lake City: Greg Kofford Books, 2012.

Radke-Moss, Andrea G. "Silent Memories of Missouri: Mormon Women and Men and Sexual Assault in Group Memory and Religious Identity." In *Mormon Women's History: Beyond Biography*, eds. Rachel Cope, Amy Easton-Flake, Keith A. Erekson, and Lisa Olsen Tait, 49–82. Lanham, MD: Fairleigh Dickinson University Press and Rowman & Littlefield, 2017.

Reeve, W. Paul. *Making Space on the Western Frontier: Mormons, Miners, and Southern Paiutes*. Urbana: University of Illinois Press, 2006.

Religion of a Different Color: Race and the Mormon Struggle for Whiteness. New York: Oxford University Press, 2015.

Rogers, Brent M. *Unpopular Sovereignty: Mormons and the Federal Management of Early Utah Territory*. Lincoln: University of Nebraska Press, 2017.

Schwartz, Regina M. *The Curse of Cain: The Violent Legacy of Monotheism.* Chicago: University of Chicago Press, 1997.

Sehat, David. *The Myth of American Religious Freedom.* New York: Oxford University Press, 2011.

Shipps, Jan. *Mormonism: The Story of a New Religious Tradition.* Urbana: University of Illinois Press, 1985.

Skousen, Royal, ed. *The Book of Mormon: The Earliest Text.* New Haven, CT: Yale University Press, 2009.

Smith, Christopher C. "Mormon Conquest: Whites and Natives in the Intermountain West, 1847–1851." Ph.D. diss., Claremont Graduate University, 2016.

Sorenson, John L. "Seasonality of Warfare in the Book of Mormon and in Mesoamerica." In *Warfare in the Book of Mormon*, eds. Stephen D. Ricks and William J. Hamblin. Salt Lake City: Deseret Book and FARMS, 1990.

Staker, Mark Lyman. *Hearken, O Ye People: The Historical Setting for Joseph Smith's Ohio Revelations.* Salt Lake City: Greg Kofford Books, 2009.

Staub, Ervin. *Overcoming Evil: Genocide, Violent Conflict, and Terrorism.* New York: Oxford University Press, 2011.

Stevenson, Russell W. "Reckoning with Race in the Book of Mormon: A Review of Literature." *Journal of Book of Mormon Studies* 27 (2018): 210–225.

Taylor, Charles. *A Secular Age.* Cambridge: Belknap Press of Harvard University Press, 2007.

Thomas, Scott K. "Violence across the Land: Vigilantism and Extralegal Justice in Utah Territory." M.A. thesis, Brigham Young University, 2010.

Thomasson, Gordon C., ed. *War, Conscription, Conscience and Mormonism.* Santa Barbara: Mormon Heritage, 1972.

Turner, John G. *Brigham Young: Pioneer Prophet*. Cambridge: Belknap Press of Harvard University Press, 2012.

Ulrich, Laurel Thatcher. *A House Full of Females: Plural Marriage and Women's Rights in Early Mormonism, 1835–1870*. New York: Alfred A. Knopf, 2017.

Underwood, Grant. *The Millenarian World of Early Mormonism*. Urbana: University of Illinois Press, 1993.

"Millennialism, Persecution, and Violence: The Mormons." In *Millennialism, Persecution, and Violence: Historical Cases*, ed. Catherine Wessinger, 43–61. Syracuse: Syracuse University Press, 2000.

Walker, Ronald W. "Sheaves, Bucklers, and the State: Mormon Leaders Respond to the Dilemmas of War." In *The New Mormon History: Revisionist Essays on the Past*, ed. D. Michael Quinn, 267–301. Salt Lake City: Signature Books, 1992.

Walker, Ronald W., Richard E. Turley Jr., and Glen M. Leonard. *Massacre at Mountain Meadows: An American Tragedy*. New York: Oxford University Press, 2008.

Weber, Max. *Politics as a Vocation*. Trans. H. H. Gerth and C. Wright Mills. Philadelphia: Fortress Press, 1965.

Weisenfeld, Judith. "Framing the Nation: Film, Religion, and American Belonging." *Journal of Mormon History* 45:2 (April 2019): 23–48.

Whitney, Orson F. *History of Utah*. 4 vols. Salt Lake City: George Q. Cannon and Sons Publishers, 1892.

Winkler, Albert Winkler. "The Circleville Massacre: A Brutal Incident in Utah's Black Hawk War." *Utah Historical Quarterly* 55:1 (Winter 1987): 4–21.

Yorgason, Ethan R. *Transformation of the Mormon Culture Region*. Urbana: University of Illinois Press, 2003.

Acknowledgments

I am grateful to the terrific staff of the Church History Department of the Church of Jesus Christ of Latter-day Saints for assistance in finding sources. I am also grateful to Claremont Graduate University, which gave me the time and resources to write this Element and was an enormously supportive home throughout my eight years as Howard W. Hunter Chair of Mormon Studies. The intellectual framework of this project can be traced to the mentorship I received many years ago from Scott Appleby, Richard Bushman, and the late Ronald Walker – three excellent historians whose work has always been characterized by generosity toward their subjects, an evenhanded yet empathetic treatment of religion and its practitioners, and deep sensitivity to the problem of violence. Although I had plenty of other projects on my plate, I couldn't turn this one down when James Lewis and Margo Kitts approached me. I am grateful for their patience and persistence in seeing this Element, and the entire series, to completion. The book's structure and arguments were vastly improved thanks to the detailed comments provided by an anonymous outside reader; any remaining errors in fact or interpretation are entirely my own.

As always, my profoundest gratitude and love go to Melissa, the ideal partner in life whose talent and creativity is a joy to behold. Finally, while writing this Element my children Finn, Rhett, Lucy, and Willa were never far from my mind. My wish is that they and their generation not only appreciate and inhabit the tradition handed down to them, but also extend their spiritual inheritance to create communities of compassion, hope, justice, and peace that the world so desperately needs. In short, I hope they build Zion.

Cambridge Elements

Religion and Violence

James R. Lewis
University of Tromsø

James R. Lewis is Professor of Religious Studies at the University of Tromsø, Norway and the author and editor of a number of volumes, including *The Cambridge Companion to Religion and Terrorism*.

Margo Kitts
Hawai'i Pacific University

Margo Kitts edits the *Journal of Religion and Violence* and is Professor and Coordinator of Religious Studies and East-West Classical Studies at Hawai'i Pacific University in Honolulu.

ABOUT THE SERIES

Violence motivated by religious beliefs has become all too common in the years since the 9/11 attacks. Not surprisingly, interest in the topic of religion and violence has grown substantially since then. This Elements series on Religion and Violence addresses this new, frontier topic in a series of ca. fifty individual Elements. Collectively, the volumes will examine a range of topics, including violence in major world religious traditions, theories of religion and violence, holy war, witch hunting, and human sacrifice, among others.

Cambridge Elements

Religion and Violence

Printed in the United States
By Bookmasters